Pikes Peak Region Traveler

THE COMPLETE TOURING GUIDE

MELISSA WALKER

WESTCLIFFE PUBLISHERS

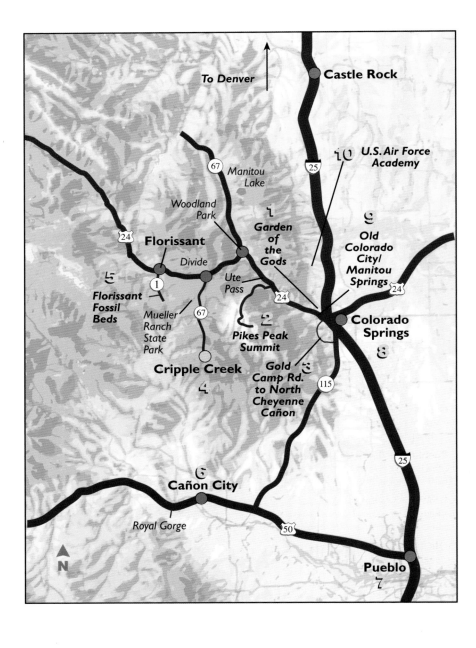

Contents

Tours

ISBN: 1-56579-292-0

Permission to use the quote from *A Bloomer Girl on Pikes Peak*, by Julia Archibald Holmes, granted by The Denver Public Library, Western History/Genealogy Department.

Permission to use the quote from *Helen Hunt Jackson's Colorado*, edited by Joe Gordon and Judy Pickle, granted by the Tutt Library, Special Collections Department, The Colorado College.

DESIGNER:

Angie Lee, Grindstone Graphics, Inc.

MAP AND GRAPHICS DESIGNER:

Jonathan Moreno

PRODUCTION MANAGER:

Harlene Finn

EDITOR:

Kiki Sayre

PUBLISHED BY:

Westcliffe Publishers, Inc.

P.O. Box 1261

Englewood, Colorado 80150

PRINTED IN:

Hong Kong, through World Print Limited

Library of Congress Cataloging-in-Publication Data

Walker, Melissa, 1950–
    The Pikes Peak region traveler / by Melissa Walker.
        p.   cm.
    ISBN 1-56579-292-0
    1. Pikes Peak Region (Colo.)—Tours.   2. Automobile travel—
Colorado—Pikes Peak Region.   I. Title.
F782.P63W35   1998
917.88'56—dc21   97-51849
                                                                                      CIP

For more information about other fine books and calendars from Westcliffe Publishers, please call your local bookstore, contact us at 1-800-523-3692, or write for our free color catalog.

Cover caption: *Pikes Peak and Garden of the Gods; photograph by Rich Buzzelli*

Acknowledgments

I wish to acknowledge those who have influenced my work, either directly or indirectly, including geologists Jeff Noblett, William Fischer, and John Lewis; biologist Richard Beidleman; southwestern literature professor Joe Gordon; paleontologist Kirk Johnson; naturalist and friend Lenore Fleck; natural history writers Curt Buchholtz and Ann Zwinger; and photographer Rich Buzzelli.

I also wish to express my appreciation to the dedicated professionals and volunteers of the Colorado Springs Parks and Recreation Department and the El Paso County Parks Department for their continuing commitment to our city's heritage of beautiful parks and natural open spaces.

To those who assisted specifically with the *Pikes Peak Region Traveler*, I wish to thank, first of all, Bob Toepfer, whose unwavering enthusiasm, support, and research assistance were invaluable in the completion of the manuscript. I also wish to thank the following for their assistance with particular chapters and the gathering of historic photos: Phil Carson of the Pikes Peak Journal, Carol Kennis of Rock Ledge Ranch Historic Site, Ginny Kiefer of Colorado College Tutt Library Special Collections, Leah Davis of the Colorado Springs Pioneers Museum Starsmore Center, Paul Idlemann of the Old Colorado City History Center, Pastor Jesse Brown, Jr., of the Payne A.M.E. Chapel, Donna Engard of the Garden Park Paleontology Society, and the staff of the Denver Public Library Western History Department and the Denver Historical Society. I would also like to thank John Fielder, Kiki Sayre, Linda Doyle, and Harlene Finn of Westcliffe Publishers for their faith in this book.

To friends through the years who have shared life's ups and downs, but find that the days spent walking, hiking, or bird watching are always good days, I thank Gretchen Arnold, Diane Elliott Lee, Dee Dehning Loomer, P. J. Wenham, Peg Hunter, Barbara Card, and John Bates.

I thank my father for his honesty and for not being too busy to stop for us to see the turtle cross the country road; my mother for her graciousness and for always appreciating the beauty of the dogwoods and the fragrance of the peace roses; my brother Rolle for being the adventurous pioneer; my brother Winston for his unpretentious love of family and every living thing; and my sister Priscilla for . . . I don't have to say because each of us knows what the other is thinking.

This book is dedicated to my husband Les, who brings love to every changing season and greets every sunrise, whether rain or snow or shine; and to our son Paul, who brings joy to every day and always tells me when the bunny is in the yard.

Introduction

When I first moved to Colorado Springs, I was an 18-year-old college student. More than anything else about that first year, I remember the thrill of waking up every morning and looking out at Pikes Peak. My parents saved the letters I wrote that year, letters full of long paragraphs about the clear, crisp fall weather, the sky that always seemed to be blue, and the new snowfall on the tops of the mountains.

Below: Mueller Ranch State Park lies to the west of Pikes Peak.

John Fielder

Having grown up comfortably enveloped in the hardwood and pine forests of Louisiana, I simply felt different in Colorado. I felt as tall as any tree as I gazed out at the expansive horizon. Views of horizons were new to me.

Here in this place, I could see where I wanted to go. I wanted to go around Cheyenne Mountain to see what was on the other side. I wanted to explore the upended rocks of the Garden of the Gods. I wanted to climb Pikes Peak.

Then, I found that wherever I went in the Pikes Peak region, I could see where I had been. On top of Mt. Cutler, I could see my dormitory back on campus. On top of Pikes Peak, I could see the cottonwood trees marking Fountain Creek's path to the Arkansas River—a river that eventually met the Mississippi and flowed by my home state. Like so many before me, I was captivated by this place. Now it is my home.

Pikes Peak Region Traveler was sparked by the hundreds of people who have asked questions about Colorado's wildlife, wildflowers, fossils, and history as they have walked along the trails with me during my years as a park naturalist. My hope is that this book will be enjoyed by everyone who wants to find out more about this radiant area of central Colorado. Alongside this region's stunning beauty are unforgettable stories of its people; inseparable from its beauty are its native plants and wildlife; and the foundations of its beauty are the rocks, canyons, mountains, and horizons.

The tours highlighted in *Pikes Peak Region Traveler* are my favorite places to explore with friends, family, and visitors. The book begins with three of Colorado Springs' most beloved landmarks—Garden of the Gods, Pikes Peak, and North Cheyenne Cañon. The next two excursions circle north and west around Pikes Peak to the celebrated mining district of Cripple Creek and to a unique paleontological site, Florissant Fossil Beds National Monument.

To investigate the southern part of the Pikes Peak region, the next two tours lead you along the Arkansas River to the Royal Gorge in Cañon City and to the city of Pueblo with its southwestern heritage. The tours that follow return to Colorado Springs to enjoy walks or drives through the historic downtown of Colorado Springs, and through Old Colorado City and Manitou Springs, both rich in history as well. Finally, the United States Air Force Academy tour heads north to the Academy's famed mountainous setting.

Together, these 10 tours take you to the area's most beautiful landscapes and cityscapes to help convey the natural and cultural history of the Pikes Peak Region. The tours do not have to be followed in chronological order, as each is complete in itself. Your exploration of the Pikes Peak Region may begin anywhere you like.

Plains to Peak Tops

The Pikes Peak region is a convergence of landforms, ecosystems, and elevations. It encompasses plains, mesas, foothills, canyons, creeks, and mountains.

The region is also a dramatic meeting ground for three of North America's major ecosystems. Here, the evergreen trees of the Rocky Mountains meet the desert cactus of the Southwest and the prairie grasses of the Great Plains.

For every 1,000-foot rise in elevation, the average temperature drops from 3 to 5 degrees Fahrenheit, depending on humidity. The climate on top of Pikes Peak is very similar to the climate above the Arctic Circle! Because of the difference in climate conditions and growing seasons at the varying altitudes, several different plant communities thrive between Pueblo (elevation 4,690 feet) and the top of Pikes Peak (elevation 14,110 feet).

The different elevations and climate conditions of this region's plains-to-peak-top topography create a patchwork-quilt effect of plant communities. These include:

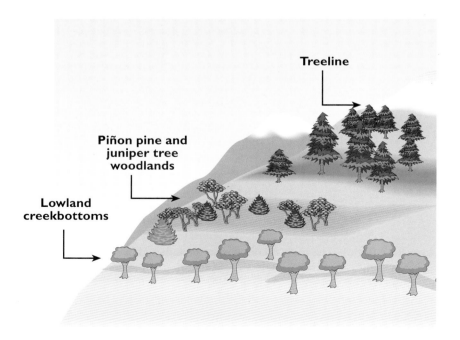

Treeline

Piñon pine and juniper tree woodlands

Lowland creekbottoms

Plains grasslands: Grasslands dominate until they meet the rising foothills. The grasses are adapted to the winds, soils, and drier climate of the prairie.

Lowland creekbottoms: Moisture-loving cottonwood and willow trees grow along the creeks, canyon floors, and drainages.

Piñon pine and juniper tree woodlands: This dry, southwestern forest thrives in the Cañon City area but does not grow much farther north than Colorado Springs.

Foothills shrublands: Mountain mahogany, scrub oak, and three-leaf sumac are the most common plants in this area of gravelly soils.

Mountain forests: Evergreen trees grow on the north-facing slopes; shrubs and grasses prefer the drier south-facing slopes.

Subalpine forests: Aspen and spruce trees flourish from 9,000 feet to treeline in this region that gets most of its moisture from snowfall.

Treeline: Trees give way to tundra at about 11,000 feet elevation. Stunted, twisted trees are evidence of the extreme climate of this wind-swept area.

Alpine tundra: "The land above the trees" is characterized by grasses, sedges, and meadows of low-growing wildflowers.

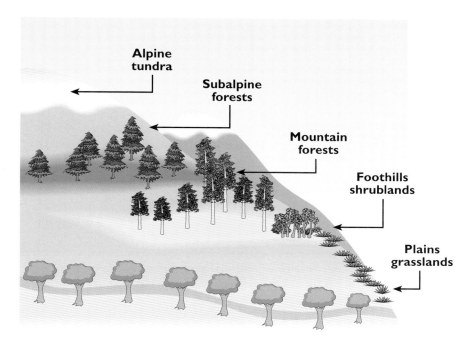

Colorado Precautions

A drive, a hike, or a walk in the mountains is a great way to spend a day. However, as with any activity, there are risks. This list of Colorado precautions describes some of the potential dangers of the mountains and how to avoid them.

High elevation and temperature: Meteorologists have been able to measure the relationship between temperature and elevation. The average temperature drops from 3 to 5 degrees Fahrenheit for every 1,000-foot rise in elevation. So, if

the temperature is 70 degrees on a summer morning in Colorado Springs (6,200 feet in elevation), the temperature will be approximately 46 degrees on top of 14,110-foot Pikes Peak (and even colder if it is windy or cloudy).

Be prepared for temperature drops and sudden weather changes by taking a warm jacket, hat, gloves, and adequate raingear anytime you venture into the mountains.

Altitude sickness: Many visitors experience some effects of Colorado's high altitude. The most common symptoms are headache, fatigue, shortness of breath, loss of appetite, and nausea. Usually, the symptoms are mild, but if any of the symptoms become acute, seek medical attention.

Drinking lots of water, getting plenty of rest, and eating extra carbohydrates usually lessen the symptoms of altitude sickness. Avoid alcohol, as it increases your chances of becoming ill. It is best to limit your time at the highest elevations, such as the top of Pikes Peak, to about an hour.

Lightning: Lightning is a real danger in the Colorado outdoors, particularly from May through September. During an approaching thunderstorm, lightning can strike as much as five times per square mile. Don't be a target.

Lightning usually strikes the highest objects in an area. As a storm approaches, avoid being caught above treeline or in any open field. Seek shelter before the rain begins to fall, as lightning can strike miles ahead of its parent cloud.

If you are unable to reach shelter, crouch down away from other tall objects. Do not seek shelter under a lone tree. Groups of people should separate and squat low to the ground.

If lightning does strike someone in your group, yell for help and start CPR immediately. Never underestimate the unpredictability and fatal power of lightning. According to the National Weather Service, it is the leading cause of weather-related deaths in the United States.

Intense sunlight: At high altitude, there is less atmosphere to filter the sun's intense rays. Many vacationers suffer unnecessarily from bad sunburns. Remember that in Colorado Springs and Cañon City, you are already more than one mile above sea level; Pueblo, too, is a high-altitude city.

Sunscreen and sunglasses are recommended for every day—even in cloud cover—and long-sleeved shirts, long pants, and hats are recommended anytime you will be out in the sun for an extended period.

Dehydration: In Colorado's low humidity, people can become dehydrated quickly. Be sure to drink more water than usual, even if you don't feel thirsty. It is a good idea to carry along a full thermos or water bottle whether you are driving or hiking.

Giardia: Even though the water of mountain streams and lakes looks crystal clear, do not drink it. Untreated Colorado water carries the parasite giardia, which can cause severe intestinal problems in humans.

Wildlife: Confrontations with wildlife are on the increase in Colorado. The best way to prevent an unpleasant encounter with a wild animal is to leave it alone. Even small chipmunks and ground squirrels can be dangerous. They sometimes bite if you try to feed them, and they are known carriers of fleas that infect humans and animals with the plague disease. A few cases of plague in humans and animals are reported almost every year in Colorado, sometimes in the Pikes Peak region.

As you hike on foothill or mountain trails, sightings of mountain lion or black bear are possible. Hiking in groups of three or more is recommended by the Colorado Mountain Club. If you or your group encounters a mountain lion or a black bear, back away and keep your eyes on the animal. Do not run or bend down. Give the animal as much space as possible to continue on its way. For more information about Colorado's wildlife and wildlife encounters, contact the Division of Wildlife (see Agency Contacts).

With a little foresight and some common sense, all of these risks can be minimized and you will be able to experience all that the Pikes Peak area has to offer.

1 Garden of the Gods

The vibrant color of the red rocks, the scenic views at every turn, the song of a canyon wren . . . the Garden of the Gods draws people for all these reasons and more. For Colorado Springs citizens, the 1,367-acre city park provides a precious place of natural beauty amid the city's rapid urbanization.

The Garden of the Gods also holds many reminders of the region's human history—ancient hearths of prehistoric hunters, the centuries-old trail of the Ute, rock signatures of gold-seekers and explorers, and homes of 19th century settlers.

The Garden is used as an outdoor classroom by geology students from schools and colleges around the country. Its 300-million-year-old rock formations, when added to the geology of Pikes Peak, reveal one of the most complete records of earth history found anywhere in the United States. Garden of the Gods Park has been designated as both a National Natural Landmark and a National Historic Place.

In addition, the Garden of the Gods is home to many different kinds of native plants and animals because of its unique location in North America. Here, the grasslands of the Great Plains meet the dry woodlands of the American Southwest, and merge with the evergreen forests of the Rocky Mountains.

To best experience this one-of-a-kind city park, plan an unhurried visit early in the day and soak in everything this beautiful place has to offer.

Garden of the Gods Park Tour

Total Mileage of Tour: 7.0 miles for motorists and bicyclists

Mileage 0.0. Set your odometer to zero at the intersection of 30th Street and Gateway Road, which features the large, sandstone entry sign to Garden of the Gods.

The Garden of the Gods Visitor Center at this intersection is the best place to begin your exploration of this famous park. Here, excellent exhibits tell the story of the park's geology, human history, native plants, and wildlife. Park staff and volunteers offer guided walks and talks several times a day year-round. Check for times at the information desk.

Mile 0.1. Note the park rules posted on your right. Remember that hiking or scrambling up the rocks is not permitted. Trained rock climbers using proper climbing equipment are allowed to climb, but they must register each year at the Garden of the Gods Visitor Center. Visitors climbing illegally or without registration may be cited and fined by the police department.

Fortunately, there are many beautiful trails for hikers and walkers to enjoy. It is best to stay on the marked trails for many reasons; one is that the rocks of the park provide great places for prairie rattlesnakes to live. Several are sighted every year.

Don't forget the 20-mile-per-hour speed

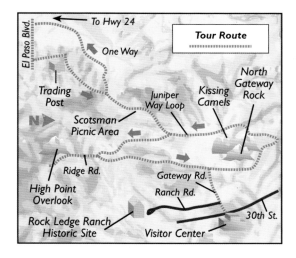

Above: North Gateway Rock and Pikes Peak define the region's rugged beauty.

limit, and that bicyclists and pedestrians will be using the marked bicycle lanes next to the shoulder of the road.

Mile 0.4. Turn right onto the one-way Juniper Way Loop. Vehicles stay to the left; bikes use the narrow lane on the right. As you proceed up the hill, the red and white sandstone rocks of the Lyons Formation tower on your left.

Rugged piñon pine and juniper trees line the lower ridges. These trees of the American Southwest are noted for their ability to withstand drought.

Mile 0.7. Turn left into the main parking lot. Before you is one of the park's most outstanding overlooks. The red sandstone spires etched against the blue sky, and the sheer size of North Gateway Rock, combine to make a very dramatic view.

The one-mile Central Garden Trail begins here. It winds between North and South Gateway Rocks and near the base of

Gray (Cathedral) Rock and Sleeping Giant Rock. Occasionally, without even leaving the parking lot, you can see Rocky Mountain bighorn sheep grazing on the ridge north of the road. This unforgettable Central Garden Trail is paved and wheelchair accessible. Also, interpretive signs are posted along the way for visitors to find out more about the wildlife, geology, and human history of the Garden of the Gods.

Turn left out of the parking lot and continue on the one-way Juniper Way Loop.

Mile 1.1. Take in the overlook view of the Central Garden area of the park with Cheyenne Mountain dominating the southern horizon.

Mile 1.4. Bear right onto Garden Drive, which leads to Balanced Rock. The road is lined with scrub oak trees and mountain mahogany

W. A. Paff, Cornell Lab of Ornithology

The Canyon Wren
A Small Bird with a Big Song

If you take an early morning walk in Garden of the Gods during spring or summer, you may be in for a special treat—the song of a canyon wren. Many people stop in their tracks when they hear the song of this small bird. The wren's haunting, flutelike call is an audible symbol of canyon country.

Of course, the wren is unaware that it makes such a big impression on humans. Like all birds, it sings primarily to attract a mate and to establish its territory. Its beautiful call is loud enough to be heard one-half mile away.

In addition to its signature song, the canyon wren can be identified by its bright, white throat and its russet tail, which usually sticks straight up. With its tiny claws, the wren is able to cling to the cliff walls as it climbs over and around rocks in search of spiders and insects to eat.

shrubs. Look out for hikers and horseback riders at the many marked pedestrian crossings.

Mile 2.2. Bear right and continue on Garden Drive.

Mile 2.7. Continue straight ahead on Garden Drive. Balanced Rock will be in sight almost immediately. Pull into the parking spaces on the right.

Balanced Rock is part of the 300-million-year-old Fountain Formation. Erosion sculpted Balanced Rock into this precarious shape as softer layers of rock near its base were eroded away, leaving its harder cap rock, or top layer.

Mile 3.1. Bear left, then turn left at the stop sign onto El Paso Boulevard. For less than one-half

Below: Sculpted red rocks stand guard at Garden of the Gods Park.

Weldon Lee

Rocky Mountain Bighorn Sheep
Living on the Edge

The Rocky Mountain bighorn sheep is the official state mammal of Colorado. Bighorns are well adapted to their rugged mountain habitat. The sheep's two-toed hooves are designed to grip rocky terrain: The back part of the hoof is padded and conforms to rock surfaces, while the front part is more flexible and can grip rocks almost like pincers. Their ability to climb steep cliffs and canyon walls is a matter of life and death when bighorns must escape from less sure-footed predators.

The Rampart Range bighorn herd comprises about 180 sheep, while the estimated size of the Pikes Peak herd farther west is 275 sheep. Visitors and citizens often spot bighorns grazing along the ridges north of Garden of the Gods Park within the city limits of Colorado Springs. Few communities can boast that the symbol of Rocky Mountain wilderness is also at home in their city!

mile, you will be outside of the park's boundary, driving through a Manitou Springs neighborhood that borders the Garden of the Gods.

Mile 3.5. Turn left at the four-way stop onto Becker's Lane. Becker's Lane leads you back into the Garden of the Gods.

Mile 3.8. Turn right into the parking lot of the Garden of the Gods Trading Post.

This gift shop/restaurant was established in 1900. All additions to the original old trading post building have matched the southwestern-style adobe architecture. Photographs in the restaurant area depict life at the trading post in the early 1900s.

Mile 4.2. Bear right onto Garden Drive. Within a short distance, you will crest a hill and see the western faces of the Garden's highest rock formations.

Rock Ledge Ranch Historic Site

Elsie and Robert Chambers
19th Century Garden of the Gods Farmers

At Rock Ledge Ranch Historic Site on the eastern edge of Garden of the Gods Park, visitors can walk into the restored home of Elsie and Robert Chambers and imagine what daily life was like in the late 1800s. Historians have carefully researched the history of the Chambers family and the events that brought them west in the spring of 1874.

Like thousands of other easterners in the 1800s, Elsie Chambers suffered from respiratory problems, and she and her husband were faced with the decision of whether or not to move to the arid West for the sake of her health. Even though there were no guarantees that Elsie would get better, the Chamberses decided to make the move. They sold their Pennsylvania farm, packed up their belongings, and took the train to Colorado with their young children.

They originally had planned to settle in the Denver area, but a fellow train passenger persuaded them to try Colorado Springs. After a summer in Colorado Springs, Elsie's health was so much better that the family decided to stay. In the fall of 1874, the Chamberses purchased 160 acres along Camp Creek—just east of the towering rocks of Garden of the Gods—and began their Colorado life.

Elsie and Robert put their energies into planting fruits and vegetables and within a few years established a successful truck farm that included six acres of asparagus and apple and cherry orchards. Rock Ledge Ranch soon became locally famous for its fresh fruits and vegetables. Even in the winter, the Chamberses delivered fresh produce from their two heated greenhouses to their largest customer, the Antlers Hotel.

In 1900, General William Jackson Palmer, their neighbor and the owner of the Antlers Hotel, offered to buy Rock Ledge Ranch. Robert and Elsie again had a big decision to make. They agreed to sell their productive land, bringing to a close two decades of farming along Camp Creek. The Chamberses could not have imagined that their industrious everyday life would be admired and studied 100 years later.

Mile 4.6. Park in the lot for the Scotsman picnic area if you have brought your lunch or a snack. An additional parking area is just ahead if the first one is full. Restrooms are located at this stop.

After parking, walk across the wooden bridge that spans a dry stream bed. Be advised that during a summer thunderstorm, this dry stream bed can quickly become a muddy torrent.

Mile 4.9. Bear right onto Juniper Way Loop. Sleeping Giant Rock looms on your left as you drive south through the piñon pines, juniper trees, and red rocks.

Mile 5.6. Bear right onto Ridge Road.

Mile 5.8. Park in the lot at High Point Overlook for a 360-degree view. To the west, 14,110-foot Pikes Peak towers over the entire landscape of nearby mountains, foothills, red rocks, and the cities of Manitou Springs and Colorado Springs. To the south, you can see the tilted red rocks of the Lyons Formation until they meet the granite of the foothills. To the north, the 90-degree angle of the highest rocks in the Garden of the Gods is now visually apparent. They were pushed into this position by the unfathomable pressure of the rising Rocky Mountains millions of years ago.

Turn left out of the parking lot back onto Ridge Road and proceed to Juniper Way Loop to continue your circular drive around the Park's most dramatic rock features.

Mile 5.9. Bear right onto Juniper Way Loop.

Mile 6.2. Pull off to the right into the gravel parking space at the top of the hill. The stone marker commemorates the Ute Pass Indian Trail, which was used for centuries by the Ute and other

Above: Hikers and mountain bikers find well-marked trails at Garden of the Gods.

William A. Fischer

Columbian Mammoth
Colorado's Prehistoric Elephant

Try to imagine a view of Pikes Peak at sunrise during the most recent Ice Age about 25,000 years ago. Glaciers of the mountain's east face are glistening in the early sunlight; cold-loving spruce and fir trees cover the mesas and foothills; and a herd of mammoths graze in the tall marsh grasses.

The Columbian mammoth, a relative of the better-known woolly mammoth, once ranged in this area of North America. With its long trunk and ivory tusks, the Columbian mammoth was similar in many ways to today's African and Indian elephants—its two living relatives. A full-grown mammoth ate about 300 pounds of grasses every day.

In 1950, a 6-foot-long mammoth tusk was excavated by a Colorado College geology class from a mesa on the west side of Colorado Springs. The tusk had been buried in gravel that was deposited by a fast-running stream of the glacial era.

American Indians as their route to and from the mountains and the plains. Today, Highway 24 follows basically the same historic trail west up Ute Pass into the higher mountains.

Mile 6.6. Turn right onto Gateway Road.

Mile 6.9. Turn right onto the entry road to Rock Ledge Ranch Historic Site. This 230-acre historic site has an admission charge. Park staff and volunteers in period costumes bring the historic site to life. Call the Ranch at 719-578-6777, or check at the Garden of the Gods Visitor Center for the historic site's exact hours, which change seasonally.

Rock Ledge Ranch Historic Site is the only living history museum in the Pikes Peak region. It depicts three distinct periods of settlement in the area. Visitors may walk through a replica of Walter Galloway's 1868 homestead cabin. Also on the walking tour is the original 1874 Rock Ledge House,

Camptosaurus The Forgotten Dinosaur

In 1995, city park naturalists began a study to find out what kind of dinosaurs may have thrived in the Garden of the Gods area. Local paleontology information had no record of any dinosaur fossil ever being found within the Park's boundaries. However, when park naturalists contacted the Denver Museum of Natural History, a museum paleontologist found information in his files that stated:

> Camptosaurus amplus: a second specimen, No. 1887, Yale Museum, consisting of portions of the skull and lower jaw. It was collected by Professor O. C. Marsh from deposits in Garden of the Gods, Colorado Springs, Colorado, in 1886.

This news was almost as exciting as discovering a brand-new dinosaur! City park staff called the Yale Museum collections manager,who confirmed that the Colorado Springs Camptosaurus skull was indeed there. Somehow, the fossil discovery had not been recorded in Colorado Springs and, eventually, was forgotten.

Over the next 18 months, arrangements were made to transport the fossil skull to Denver so that the Denver Museum of Natural History staff could make a cast (a precise replica) of the original dinosaur skull. In 1997, the Camptosaurus fossil replica was given to the city of Colorado Springs. It is a rare gift, with an ancient and a modern story.

The Camptosaurus—meaning bent lizard—lived during the Jurassic era about 150 million years ago. It was medium-sized as far as dinosaurs go, weighing about 1,200 pounds and measuring about 23 feet long from head to tail. Its head was elongated with a beak that was toothless in front and had tightly packed blunt teeth in the back—evidence of a plant eater.

Camptosaurus fossils have been discovered in western North America, Europe, and Australia. A complete skeleton was excavated from Dinosaur National Monument in Utah, and fossil evidence of the dinosaur has also been found in Cañon City, Colorado.

An excellent mural of the Camptosaurus living in its Jurassic world can be viewed at the Garden of the Gods Visitor Center. The huge painting depicts a time in our Earth's history when the climate, plants, and animals were very different from those of today.

Colorado Springs Pioneers Museum

Charles Elliott Perkins
Garden of the Gods Donor

Many people expect to pay an entry fee when they visit Garden of the Gods Park. With its stunning scenery and many international visitors, it seems like a national park. Yet, Garden of the Gods is a free city park. How the Garden became a public park is a story of friendship and of children fulfilling their father's dream.

In 1879, William Jackson Palmer convinced his good friend Charles Perkins (president of the Chicago, Burlington and Quincy Railroad) to buy several hundred acres of red rock spires and piñon-covered foothills known as Garden of the Gods. A few years later, Perkins wrote to Palmer of his intention to donate his 480-acre Garden of the Gods property to the city of Colorado Springs. Perkins undoubtedly was influenced by Palmer, who had already donated over 1,000 acres of his own land to become public city park lands.

Unfortunately, Perkins died in 1907 before he had officially arranged for the Garden to become a public park. But Perkins's four daughters and two sons, knowing their father's wish, deeded the beloved land to the city of Colorado Springs on December 22, 1909, with the stipulation that it remain "free to all the world."

Thanks to the Perkins heirs, and to the friendship between Palmer and Perkins, citizens and visitors from all over the world can enjoy this special place and contemplate its sheer beauty—without an entry fee.

one of the oldest buildings in Colorado Springs that is open to the public, and the 1907 Orchard House, a country estate built by William Jackson Palmer for his sister-in-law and her family.

Mile 7.0. At the intersection of 30th Street and Gateway Road, you are back where you started and have completed the Garden of the Gods tour. If you didn't go to the Visitor Center at the beginning of your trip, plan to stop at the end of your tour to take advantage of the excellent film and exhibits that tell the story of the rocks in this unusual park.

Red-Tailed Hawk
Riding the Air Waves

Weldon Lee

Red-tailed hawks have broad wings, 4-foot wingspans, and rounded tails that enable them to catch rising currents of warm air. They ride these air currents, called thermals, to soar high in the sky on the lookout for prey.

From its "perch" in the sky, the hawk uses its phenomenal eyesight—eight times better than human sight—to spot a mouse scurrying on the ground one-half mile away. The red-tail then swoops down and grasps the mouse in its talons. Other favorite foods of this large bird are squirrels, rabbits, large grasshoppers, and even an occasional snake.

The red-tailed hawk is one of the easiest hawks to identify with its reddish tail, and is one of the most common hawks in the Pikes Peak region. Pairs of red-tails use the same territory and nesting area year after year, and usually mate for life.

In many parts of Colorado Springs, you can see this impressive bird almost daily. In natural parks and near the foothills, the hawks are likely to be either soaring or perching in tall trees as they survey the landscape for any movement by their unsuspecting prey.

2

Pikes Peak Summit

On the summit of Pikes Peak you are standing where the earth meets the sky—and you are standing where the Great Plains meet the Rocky Mountains, and the arid Southwest reaches to the snow-laden evergreen forests. On a clear day you can see 100 miles in all directions.

Pikes Peak's first recorded names chronicle part of this region's compelling history. According to today's Southern Ute tribal historians, Sun Mountain is their descriptive name for Pikes Peak. As the easternmost 14,000-foot peak in Colorado, it is the first to catch the sun's rays at dawn.

In the late 1700s, Spaniards traveling in colonial New Mexico called the peak El Capitán, meaning "the captain." Early in the next century, Zebulon Pike labeled the mountain Grand Peak. Then in 1820, explorer Stephen Long named it James Peak after Edwin James, a member of his expedition who successfully climbed the mountain. By the 1850s Pikes Peak was generally accepted as the official name.

As you drive up Pikes Peak today, you are following the route of the carriage road that Katharine Lee Bates took to the top of the mountain in 1893. The view inspired her to write a poem about "spacious skies" and "purple mountain majesties" that became the song "America the Beautiful."

The Pikes Peak Highway is open year-round, weather and road conditions permitting. If you are in doubt, call ahead (see Agency Contacts). On your drive, you will be climbing from an elevation of 6,200 feet in Colorado Springs to more than 14,000 feet at the summit, an elevation gain of almost 8,000 feet! Be prepared for a breathtaking adventure.

The Pikes Peak Summit Tour

Total Mileage of Tour: 37.1 miles

Those who are prepared for the drive to the summit of Pikes Peak will experience an exhilarating trip they won't soon forget. However, it is important to know the risks of high-altitude travel. To safely drive to 14,000 feet, first consider these questions:

- Do you have a fear of heights? If so, it would probably be better to let someone else do the driving, or to ride the cog railway.

- How is your health? If you have a history of heart or breathing difficulties, a trip to the top of Pikes Peak is not recommended. Infants younger than two months old may also have breathing difficulties at 14,000 feet.

- How are your brakes? Your vehicle should be in good operating condition to make this drive.

- Have you packed a jacket? The temperature on top of the mountain is usually from 24 to 40 degrees cooler than in Colorado Springs. If you leave Colorado Springs on a 75-degree summer morning, it may be 45 degrees or colder at the summit. Often, in wind or clouds, it will be even colder. Snow is common every month of the year on the top of Pikes Peak.

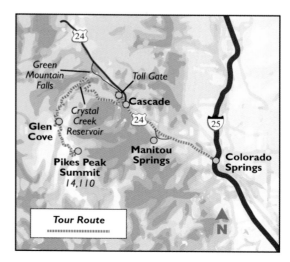

- How is the weather? To reduce the chances of driving in a thunderstorm, make the trip up Pikes Peak first thing in the morning. If you begin soon after the tollgate opens, you will usually be ahead of the frequent summer rainstorms and most of the traffic. If it is a rare stormy morning, plan your drive for the following day. Always take cover from lightning.

- What will you do if you need help? If you find that you unexpectedly have health concerns, flag down the Pikes Peak Highway Patrol or alert any staff person at Glen Cove (halfway to the top) or at the Summit House. They can assist you and summon emergency-trained personnel.

Directions to the start: At the intersection of Interstate 25 and Highway 24 in Colorado Springs (Interstate Exit 141), drive west on Highway 24 into the mountains for 9.4 miles.

Turn left off Highway 24 at the well-marked Pikes Peak Highway sign and follow the signs for about one mile to the Pikes Peak Highway entrance.

Stop at the Pikes Peak tollgate to pay the per-person toll fee and to receive a map of the drive. Note the highway driving tips on the brochure map that will help you and your vehicle safely climb to 14,110 feet and back.

Set your odometer to 0.0 at the tollgate.

Mile 1.0. To the left you can look down Ute Pass and see where the foothills meet the plains and Colorado Springs. Some of the colorful summer flowers that line the road along this stretch are blue penstemon, wild rose, pink wild geranium, and the salmon-to-red blossoms of scarlet gilia.

Mile 5.3. Exhibits at the Crystal Creek Reservoir Visitor Center describe Pikes Peak and its plants and animals. Restrooms are a short walk to the right along the trail to the fishing dock.

Opposite: Spacious skies and views await visitors to the summit of Pikes Peak.

The view of Pikes Peak's north face is definitely worth a stop. In summer, light-green

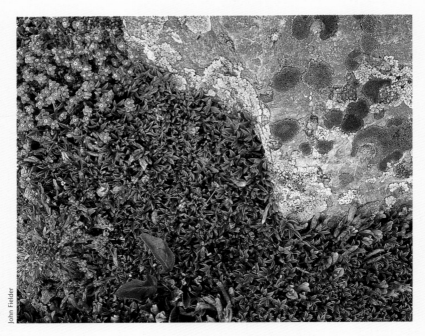

John Fielder

Alpine Forget-Me-Not

When Julia Archibald Holmes climbed Pikes Peak in 1858, she wrote of finding "dozens of tiny blue flowers most bewitchingly beautiful." Undoubtedly, she was describing the alpine forget-me-not flowers.

Low-growing and with five rounded petals, these high alpine tundra flowers are an added highlight on a trip up Pikes Peak.

aspen trees are interspersed with darker evergreen trees on the peak's lower shoulders, with the massive granite summit dominating the view. In the foreground, Crystal Creek Reservoir often mirrors the mountain scene.

Pikes Peak has very little topsoil, so just about everywhere you look or walk, you can see the pinkish Pikes Peak granite that the mountain is made of. If you look closely at the rocks in the gravelly soil, you will be able to see the three primary minerals that make up this granite—reddish pink feldspar, grayish white quartz, and shiny black mica. The high percentage of feldspar gives Pikes Peak granite its recognizable pink color.

Mile 9.0. As you gain altitude on the steep switchback curves, the views to the north reach beyond the reservoir lakes and the town of Woodland Park to the forested hills of the Rampart Range and the high peaks west of Denver.

Mile 10.4. This is the site of the former Pikes Peak Ski Area, which closed in the mid-1980s. Trees are beginning to grow back in the old ski runs.

Mile 11.6. At Glen Cove Inn, restrooms, a picnic area, a gift shop, and a snack bar are available. This is good place to stop on your way down the mountain to let your brakes cool off, if necessary. If you have brought a picnic lunch or snack, there are picnic tables in the forest across the road from Glen Cove.

Below: People of all ages are captivated by the beauty of Pikes Peak.

Garden of the Gods Visitor Center

From the picnic area of Glen Cove, you can see bristlecone pines and other gnarled trees growing on the ridge. Their growth is stunted by the high-altitude conditions and shaped by the prevailing winds. The twisted trees at tree limit are sometimes called krummholtz, a German word meaning "crooked wood."

Soon after leaving Glen Cove, you will climb to the land of alpine tundra, leaving the trees behind.

Mile 14.7. If there are no approaching storms, the gravel turnout at Devil's Playground is a good place to park and take a short walk to view the tiny alpine wildflowers of Pikes Peak that usually bloom from mid-June until mid-August. Pink moss campion, blue sky pilot, purple saxifrage, and alpine forget-me-nots are among the flowers hardy enough to grow above treeline. Some of these slow-growing flowers are

Julia Archibald Holmes
An Independent and Adventurous Woman

Born in 1838, Julia Archibald Holmes was raised by parents who were strong advocates for freedom. Her mother was a firm believer in voting rights for women and was a friend of the renowned women's rights leader Susan B. Anthony. Julia's father believed so strongly that slavery should be abolished that he moved his family from Massachusetts to Kansas to champion the cause of its becoming a free state. Runaway slaves found shelter and safety at the Archibalds' Kansas home, which became a stop on the Underground Railroad.

With this family background, Julia, not surprisingly, chose adventure over a routine life. In 1858, when Julia was only 20 years old, she and her like-minded husband, James, joined a wagon train and headed west. Their Lawrence, Kansas, party included 46 other men, only one other woman, and 11 ox-drawn wagons.

For the arduous trek, Julia set aside traditional women's attire and donned a bloomer outfit. Not only was it more practical, it was also the official uniform of the 1850s women's rights activists. In this sensible garment, Julia walked with the men beside the wagons all the way to the base of Pikes Peak.

After three weeks of camping by Fountain Creek near today's Manitou Springs, Julia and James set out to climb Pikes Peak with two men. Still strong from their overland walk from Kansas, the Holmes party forged their own route up the steep and rocky slopes, as no trail existed in 1858.

After five days of climbing, exploring, and camping along the way, the party reached the top of the peak. "Nearly everyone tried to discourage me from attempting it, but I believed I should succeed; and now, here I am and I feel that I would not have missed this glorious sight for anything at all," Julia later exclaimed in a letter to her mother.

Soon after their successful climb, Julia and James headed south to Santa Fe and established their home. Julia had four children and became a corresponding writer for the *New York Tribune*, while James served as the Secretary of the Territory of New Mexico.

Denver Public Library

After 12 years in the West, the Holmes family moved to Washington, D.C., where Julia advocated for women's voting rights as her mother had done. Julia died in 1887 at the age of 49, long before women finally won the right to vote in 1920.

Julia is credited as the first woman to scale Pikes Peak. In light of the rest of her life, Julia's daring 1858 climb was an exclamation point in a lifetime that reflected the American values of freedom, independence, and equality for all.

Old Colorado City History Center

Zebulon Montgomery Pike
An Early 19th Century Explorer

After the Louisiana Purchase in 1803, President Thomas Jefferson dispatched the Lewis and Clark expedition and Zebulon Montgomery Pike's expedition to survey and map the boundless western regions that had suddenly become part of the United States.

From 1804 to 1806, as the Lewis and Clark expedition was exploring the vast Missouri and Columbia River systems, Pike was assigned to explore two other regions.

Pike's first assignment, in 1805, was to explore the Mississippi River from St. Louis to northern Minnesota. His next assignment, in 1806, was to trace the Arkansas and Red Rivers to their source. This overland expedition brought Pike into present-day Colorado.

circumpolar, meaning they grow in tundra regions all around the Northern Hemisphere—such as in Alaska, Siberia, the Alps, and the Himalaya Mountains.

It is very important to stay on the old roadbed trail so as not to disturb the tundra flowers. They are vulnerable and take many years to grow back if trampled.

Mile 18.4. The summit of Pikes Peak is a place of views—and usually wind, too. The view to the east features the Great Plains and extends to the horizon. To the south are the Sangre de Cristo

Pike kept day-by-day accounts of his expeditions. In his journals, he described what he ate each day, what hardships he and his men encountered, the American Indians he met, his horse's behavior, and all that he saw on his journeys. In his journal entry for November 15, 1806, he wrote about a mountain or a blue cloud in the distance. This was his first view of the mountain that we know of today as Pikes Peak, the mountain that Pike called "Grand Peak."

On November 24, Pike and three other men left their party camped near the Arkansas River (at the location of present-day Pueblo), and hiked north toward the peak. Following two days of hiking, they had only reached the base of the mountain. After two more days of climbing, they were stopped by severe cold (minus 4 degrees F.) and waist-deep snow. It took two more days to return to their party camped at the river. The expedition then continued on up the Arkansas.

Even though Pike was unsuccessful in his attempt to climb the Grand Peak, it was eventually named in his honor. Pike was killed in the War of 1812, just six years after his western expedition, at the age of 34. He did not live long enough to know that the Grand Peak was renamed after him, or that Pikes Peak would become one of the most famous mountains in the world.

Mountains, usually snow-capped; to the west are the mountains of the Sawatch Range and the Continental Divide; to the north are Longs Peak and the Front Range mountains.

On the east side of the Summit House, you may see other travelers arriving on the cog railway, and a few hikers completing their 12.6-mile climb from Manitou Springs. Far below is Colorado Springs, with its downtown streets laid out in a checkerboard grid.

In the summer months, a park naturalist from the Colorado Springs Parks and Recreation Department or from the U.S. Forest Service is usually on hand to answer your questions. At the snack bar, it is a tradition to sample the high-altitude donuts. They are a rare specialty on the top of a 14,000-foot mountain!

Remember to drive in low gear on your way down Pikes Peak.

Mile 22.2. If you decided not to stop at Devil's Playground on your way up, here is another opportunity.

John Fielder

Bristlecone Pine

The Rocky Mountain bristlecone pine grows only in the mountains of Colorado, New Mexico, and northern Arizona. On the slopes of Pikes Peak, bristlecones are one of the only trees that can survive at 11,000 feet. At this elevation, bristlecones are sculpted by the high, unceasing winds and are sometimes called "flag trees."

Bristlecone pines are identified by their 2-inch-long needles that are sprinkled with white dots of resin. The pine cones take three years to mature and are covered by sharp bristles—hence the tree's name. The slow-growing trees may live to be over 1,000 years old, making them among the oldest living things on earth.

Mile 25.3. At Glen Cove Inn the Pikes Peak Highway Patrol checks for hot brakes as you descend the mountain.

Mile 37.1. Pass the tollgate. As you leave Pikes Peak, it is probably easier now to understand why Zebulon Pike declared that the mountain would never be climbed!

Return to Highway 24 and turn right to make your way back to Colorado Springs. It is a 10.5-mile drive from the tollgate back to the intersection of Highway 24 and Interstate 25.

Yellow-Bellied Marmot
A True Hibernator

Les Goss

Closely related to the eastern United States' groundhog or woodchuck, the yellow-bellied marmot is common in rocky areas up to about 12,000 feet. The marmot's two nicknames, "rock chuck" and "whistle pig," are telling—it lives in rock fields, has a rounded shape, and makes a loud, piercing call.

The marmot hibernates during the winter, sleeping for almost nine months. To successfully hibernate, a marmot must eat enough during the short summer to build up its body-fat reserves to 60 percent of its body weight.

When the marmot begins hibernating, its body temperature drops to within a few degrees of freezing and its heart and breathing rates slow down. By living on its body fat, the marmot survives the long, high-altitude winter.

Often on summer days, you can observe the marmot lumbering about the tundra, eating its fill of grasses and wildflowers as it instinctively prepares for winter.

3

Gold Camp Road

W*hile traversing this mountainous route by train in 1901, then Vice President Theodore Roosevelt reportedly exclaimed, "This is the trip that bankrupts the English language!" Visitors today may feel the same.*

Driving along the old railroad grade of the Short Line Railroad and through two tunnels dynamited out of solid granite, it becomes obvious that railroads were critical to the commerce of the goldfields. The Short Line was one of three railroad routes that linked the Cripple Creek gold-mining district with the outside world.

Thoughts of railroads and history give way to waterfalls and poetry as you enter North Cheyenne Cañon. North and South Cheyenne Cañons were an inspiration to Helen Hunt Jackson, an acclaimed poet and novelist in the late 1800s. Her essays on her beloved canyons, wildflowers, and waterfalls are still in print, assembled in a book entitled Bits of Travel at Home.

Fortunately, North Cheyenne Cañon looks much the same as when Teddy Roosevelt and Helen Hunt Jackson saw it. As a Colorado Springs city park, it is protected from development and will continue to inspire travelers and history buffs, presidents, and poets.

Gold Camp Road and North Cheyenne Cañon Tour

Total Mileage of Tour: 14.2 *miles for motorists and bicyclists*

Mileage 0.0. At the intersection of Highway 24 and 21st Street in Colorado Springs, set your odometer to zero. This intersection at 21st Street is about 1.6 miles west of Interstate 25 on Highway 24.

Turn left (south) off of Highway 24 onto 21st Street. Note the Van Briggle Pottery Building on the right. It was originally built as the roundhouse for the Colorado Midland Railroad, one of two railroads that connected Colorado Springs to the goldfields of Cripple Creek at the turn of the 20th century.

On the left side, look for the huge smokestack. It is all that is left of a gold processing mill that thrived during the 1890s and early 1900s.

Mile 0.7. Turn right (west) onto Lower Gold Camp Road. You are now driving on the old railroad bed of the Short Line Railroad that led from the goldfields of Cripple Creek to the processing mills of Old Colorado City. After the Cripple Creek heyday, the Short Line was abandoned and eventually converted into a road for automobiles. Gold Camp Road climbs at a

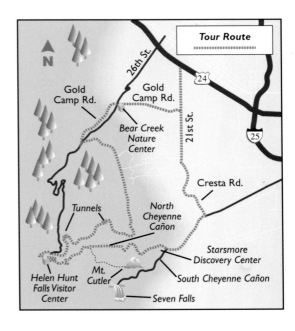

Opposite: North Cheyenne Cañon is a favorite Colorado Springs retreat.

4 percent grade, providing easy access to the rugged terrain and beautiful views of North Cheyenne Cañon.

Mile 1.8. Turn left (south) onto Bear Creek Road. This short departure from Gold Camp Road will lead you to Bear Creek Nature Center. The entrance to the Center is within sight on the left as soon as you drive down Bear Creek Road. The facility offers excellent exhibits and programs on the plants and animals of this part of Colorado. Park naturalists and volunteers can answer your questions and provide bird checklists for avid bird watchers. Maps are available that describe the hiking trails that wind along Bear Creek and the foothills. One trail is wheelchair accessible.

Turn right (north) out of the Nature Center parking lot and drive back up the hill to resume your journey on Gold Camp Road.

Mile 2.3. Turn left (west) at the intersection onto Gold Camp Road. As you follow Gold Camp Road for the next 2 miles, the road begins to climb, offering expansive views to the east. You can see over the cityscape of Colorado Springs to the broad prairie and eastern horizon beyond.

Most of the trees along this stretch are ponderosa pines, which thrive in the gravelly soils and intense sunshine of this elevation. The paved road will give way to a well-maintained gravel road.

Mile 5.0. Pull off the road into the informal gravel parking area on the right. Now the views open up to beautiful Cheyenne Mountain, North Cheyenne Cañon, and evergreen forests. On the east-facing slope of Cheyenne Mountain you will be able to see the stone tower of Will Roger's Shrine. Will Rogers was a famous actor and humorist from the early 1900s but met an untimely death in a plane crash. This monument near the mouth of Cheyenne Cañon was built by Spencer Penrose, who made his fortune in mining. Penrose counted Rogers as a close friend.

Far below, you can see the floor of the canyon and the curvy road that parallels North Cheyenne Creek, where you will be driving later on this tour.

The Fragrant and Colorful Wild Rose

Cheyenne Mountain holds canyons where one can climb among fir trees and roses and clematis and columbine . . . to wild pools and cascades in which snow-fed brooks tumble and leap.

—*Helen Hunt Jackson, 1876*

The wildflowers that Helen Hunt Jackson described more than 100 years ago bring color and fragrance to Cheyenne Cañon today. The fragrant pink flowers of the wild rose bush are found throughout the southern Rockies. They usually bloom in June in the shade of evergreen or aspen trees. In late summer, red rose hips (fruits) develop and are used by many birds and mammals as a source of food during winter.

Bear Facts

Weldon Lee

Colorado black bears are not very large and are not usually black. Most of our black bears are about 3 feet tall at the shoulder and are actually a shade of brown.

Contrary to the image of bears as hungry meat eaters, black bears eat mostly plants. Ninety percent of their diet is made up of berries, fruits, nuts, and leaves. It is true that bears love honey, and in recent years Colorado Springs' beekeepers have had to move their beehives outside of the territory of local bears.

In preparation for winter, bears eat almost constantly, consuming nearly 20,000 calories per day! Extra body fat is essential for their winter survival, since bears do not leave their dens to eat or drink for several months.

Although black bears sleep deeply all winter, they are not considered true hibernators because their body temperatures drop only a few degrees. True hibernators, such as marmots and ground squirrels, have much colder winter body temperatures—just a few degrees above freezing.

Black bears are occasionally sighted in the foothills and in some neighborhoods on the west side of Colorado Springs. Sometimes, a backyard hummingbird feeder is raided by a bear that is attracted to the sweet smell of sugary water.

Mile 5.6. The first railroad tunnel comes into view. During the early 1900s, two trains per day chugged up and down this railway. The last run of the Short Line Railroad was in 1920. In 1924, the rails were removed and the roadbed was converted for use by automobiles.

Mile 6.6. Drive through the second railroad tunnel.

Mile 7.1. Pull off on the right side of the road. This stop offers a great view of Silver Cascade Falls, one of several waterfalls in North Cheyenne Cañon. You can also see Gold Camp Road continuing its gradual climb up and around the mountains.

Bear left at the intersection with the pavement, and drive down the hill on paved North Cheyenne Road.

Mile 7.9. Park at the Helen Hunt Falls Visitor Center. The small visitor center and bookstore are usually open during the summer months and provide information about author and poet Helen Hunt Jackson and the plants and animals of North Cheyenne Cañon. Only a few steps lead you to the base of Helen Hunt Falls, named for the poet, and to the bridge overlooking the waterfalls. In the summer, hummingbirds are very common in this cool area near the creek.

The trail leading from Helen Hunt Falls to Silver Cascade Falls is quite steep and should be attempted only by strong hikers.

Mile 8.0. Pull off the road at the picnic area if you have brought a lunch or a snack. This pleasant picnic area is shaded by towering Douglas fir trees and serenaded by the rushing waters of North Cheyenne Creek. Chipmunks

Helen Hunt Jackson
An Author and Activist

A new life awaited 43-year-old Helen Hunt when she stepped off the train in Colorado Springs in 1873. The life she had left behind in Massachusetts had been filled with sadness. Her infant son died, followed by the death of her husband, and then the loss of her beloved nine-year-old son Rennie from diphtheria.

At the urgings of her concerned friends, Helen began to write about her grief; and at the encouragement of her doctor, she decided to go west.

Soon after her move to Colorado Springs, Helen Hunt's energy for life returned. She began to take long walks and carriage rides, then sold accounts of her travels to magazines back East. Helen's renewed joy is reflected in her emotional descriptions about Colorado Springs:

> Are there many spots on earth where the whole rounded horizon is thus full of beauty and grandeur, and where . . . is added the subtle and indescribable spell of the rarefied air and light of six thousand feet above the sea?

Within two years, she married William Sharpless Jackson, who shared her love for excursions into the mountains. He was also a successful businessman in his work as treasurer of William Jackson Palmer's Denver & Rio Grande Railroad Company.

Helen Hunt Jackson's compassion for others, heightened by her own life's sadness, eventually led her to become a very vocal critic of the unjust treatment of American Indians. In 1881 and 1882, she wrote a controversial book entitled *A Century of Dishonor* and spent five months in southern California documenting the mistreatment of American Indians in the old Spanish missions of the area. Two years later, Helen wrote the novel *Ramona,* a poignant love story about two mission Indians. Historians credit these two books with calling national attention to the plight of American Indians.

Colorado College Tutt Library

Helen Hunt Jackson will always be remembered locally for her fresh and detailed descriptions of the landscape, sky, and flowers of this mountainous country she came to love.

Colorado Springs Pioneers Museum

Spencer Penrose
An Influential Entrepreneur

Young and energetic, Spencer Penrose (pictured center) arrived in Colorado Springs in 1892 hoping to make a name for himself and to match the success of his three talented older brothers. As a Harvard University graduate and son of a well-respected Philadelphia family, Spencer had not yet found his niche. Meanwhile, his older brothers had already succeeded in their respective careers of politics, medicine, and geology.

Spencer came to Colorado Springs at the suggestion of his brother, Dick, who was a consulting geologist in Colorado. Also, Spencer's childhood friend, Charles L.

Tutt, was already involved in real estate and mining claims in the area. On Spencer's very first day in Colorado Springs, he seized the opportunity to go into business with Charles. It was a partnership that lasted throughout their lives.

The partners' first successful venture eventually led them both to great wealth. Their Cripple Creek gold-mining claim, the Cash On Delivery Mine, lived up to its name and sold for $250,000. This helped fund their second business, the Colorado-Philadelphia Reduction Mill, and later other mills, which processed gold from the Cripple Creek and Victor mines.

Money from the gold processing mills provided the capital needed for their third and most profitable business of all—copper mining. Spencer received financial backing from his father and three older brothers to form the Utah Copper Company with Charles Tutt and one other partner. This new company mined and processed copper from Bingham Canyon, Utah. Again, luck and talent were on his side, and in a few years when Utah Copper merged with Kennecott Copper, all the investors were handsomely rewarded.

Now that Spencer had made his fortune, he focused his incredible energy and money on new pursuits closer to home. He built the Pikes Peak Highway in 1915 and established the Cheyenne Mountain Zoo in 1916. Influenced by his civic-minded wife, Julie, he donated $250,000 to the Broadmoor Arts Academy, the predecessor of the Colorado Springs Fine Arts Center.

Spencer is best remembered by Colorado Springs citizens for building the landmark Broadmoor Hotel in 1918 and for establishing the El Pomar Foundation in 1937, two years before his death. This charitable foundation donates millions of dollars in grants every year.

and chickaree squirrels are often seen scurrying here in their forested domain.

Mile 9.0. Pull off to the right into the angled parking of Mt. Cutler Trailhead. This is a favorite hike with locals because it is so close to town, yet gives the impression of being far off in the mountains. It also has great views of Seven Falls, Cheyenne

Weldon Lee

Broad-Tailed Hummingbird
An Iridescent Bundle of Energy

Everyone loves hummingbirds. The tiny birds are bundles of energy that ricochet through the air with iridescent feathers glinting in the sun. They are the only birds that can fly backwards or beat their wings more than 50 times per second.

Part of the fun of a Colorado summer is watching a broad-tailed hummingbird in action. At hummingbird feeders, the birds are so intent on their food that they will allow curious humans to come very close. You can see the bird's thin tongue reaching in and out to gather nectar, and can feel the air moving from its incessantly beating wings.

The broad-tailed hummingbird is sometimes mistaken for the ruby-throated hummingbird because of its metallic green back and solid red throat. However, the ruby-throated is found in the eastern United States, while the broad-tailed is quite common in Colorado and the Southwest.

The season of hummingbirds is short-lived. In late summer, the "hummers" migrate back to Mexico and Central America on their endless search for blooming flowers that provide life-sustaining nectar.

Mountain, Will Roger's Shrine, and the city giving way to the eastern plains.

It is definitely a hike, rather than a walk, with an elevation gain of about 600 feet. Round-trip, the trail is nearly 2 miles long.

Close to the top, hike carefully on the gravelly rock. There are no handrails on this

Below: Rushing waters of North Cheyenne Creek cascade over Helen Hunt Falls.

Bob Toepfer

Weldon Lee

mountain trail, so stay a safe distance away from cliffs and steep drop-offs.

Along the hike, listen for the chimes of Will Roger's Shrine and the natural sounds of the birds, the wind in the trees, and the rushing water. After feeling the fresh breezes and taking in the distant views of this area, it is easy to understand why North and South Cheyenne Cañons were so loved by Helen Hunt Jackson more than a century ago.

The Chattering Chickaree Pine Squirrel

Few people can hike through our mountain forests without being scolded by a chickaree pine squirrel, a very noisy and territorial little gray squirrel!

The chickaree gnaws through pine cones to reach its preferred food—conifer seeds. Usually this squirrel has a favorite feeding tree where it eats and drops leftover pieces of pine cones. The shredded cones accumulate into huge piles, called middens, that are sometimes several feet across. Very large middens are evidence that several generations of chickarees have used the same feeding area for many years.

In summer and fall, the chickaree gathers whole pine cones and buries them in the midden to serve as its winter food supply. On cold winter days, the well-prepared squirrel retrieves and eats a few of its stored cones.

As you walk or picnic in the forests of Cheyenne Cañon, look for a chickaree's midden at the base of an evergreen fir tree. And if you hear a squirrel chattering at you long before you can see it, no doubt it is a chickaree.

Mile 10.4. Stop in at the Starsmore Discovery Center on the right. Once a comfortable home, this beautiful facility was donated to the city by the Starsmore family. Today, it is a treasured visitor center where Colorado Springs citizens and visitors enjoy finding out more about the history and ecology of North Cheyenne Cañon.

Note: To see additional beautiful waterfalls, Seven Falls in South Cheyenne Cañon is a very short distance from Starsmore Discovery Center. From the Discovery Center simply head west up South Cheyenne Cañon Road. Expect to pay an entry fee for Seven Falls.

Return to Cheyenne Cañon Boulevard and continue driving east to the stoplight at Cresta Road.

Turn left (north) onto Cresta Road and drive 2.7 miles back to Highway 24. Cresta Road becomes 21st Street as you drive north. Once you intersect Highway 24, you have completed the entire 14.2-mile loop. As you enter the noisy city traffic, don't forget the cool breezes, sweeping views, and waterfalls of North Cheyenne Cañon.

4 Cripple Creek/Mueller Ranch State Park

Gold mines and railroads are at the heart of Cripple Creek's history. In 1890, prospector and cowboy Bob Womack found gold at Poverty Gulch on the southwestern slopes of Pikes Peak and set off a dozen years of gold frenzy in the area.

Before Womack's gold discovery, the population of Cripple Creek and the surrounding hills was under 500. By 1902, the population had mushroomed to more than 40,000 people supporting 41 assay offices, eight newspapers, two opera houses, three railroads, a stock exchange, and 70 saloons.

Cripple Creek was Colorado's last gold strike, but it was also its biggest. In 1902, Cripple Creek was the leader in the world's gold production. In today's dollars, it is estimated that Cripple Creek has produced $7 billion worth of gold.

Although the boom escalated for only 12 years, Cripple Creek made its mark on the history of the state and the nation. This tour takes you deep inside a gold mine, on a narrow-gauge railroad, along Cripple Creek's main street, and finally to Mueller Ranch State Park, featuring some of Colorado's other natural resources, such as evergreen forests, native wildlife, and outdoor recreation.

Cripple Creek and Mueller Ranch State Park Tour

Total Mileage of Tour: 90.0 miles

Mile 0.0. Set your odometer to zero at the intersection of Interstate 25 and Highway 24, Interstate Exit 141. Drive west toward the mountains on Highway 24.

Mile 5.3. Look to the right as the road crosses Williams Canyon. In view up the canyon are the buildings that serve as the entrance to the Cave of the Winds, an unusual limestone cave system. On the left, the town of Manitou Springs nestles in the foothills of Pikes Peak.

Mile 6.3. Note the railroad tunnels on the left side of the high-way. The tunnels mark the route of the Colorado Midland Railroad, which once linked Colorado

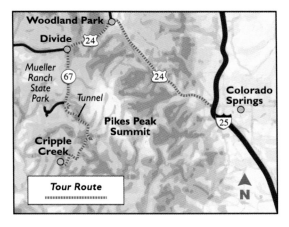

Springs and Manitou Springs to the mountain mining towns and Grand Junction.

Mile 17.5. The view from the town of Woodland Park of Pikes Peak's craggy north face is among the best in the region.

Mile 25.0. Turn left (south) on Highway 67 at the stoplight in the town of Divide.

Mile 29.0. Note the entrance to Mueller Ranch State Park. This is a recommended stop on your return from Cripple Creek.

Bob Toepfer

Above: The Cripple Creek and Victor Railroad takes visitors back in time to the gold rush days.

Mile 34.3. This railroad tunnel is a remnant of the Midland Terminal Railroad, a spur railroad that connected Cripple Creek to the Colorado Midland Railroad at the town of Divide, and hence to the outside world.

Mile 41.5. Stop at the scenic overlook to take in the panorama of the historic Cripple Creek gold district and the Sangre de Cristo and Sawatch mountain ranges on the southwestern and western horizons. "Glory holes" dot the hills surrounding Cripple Creek. These are remnants of shallow mines dug over a century ago by miners hoping to find a rich vein of gold.

Weldon Lee

The Coyote
More Often Heard Than Seen

A slight movement catches your eye. At the edge of a clump of scrub oaks is a coyote, stalking its next meal. Suddenly the coyote pounces, catches its prey, then disappears into the thick brush.

If you glimpse a coyote in the daytime, you are lucky. Their gray-and-brown fur blends well with the terrain, and they are most active at night. If you are near natural parks, the outskirts of the city, or in the mountains, you may hear coyotes at night. Particularly on moonlit nights, they howl, yip, and bark to unite their family groups. Coyotes are named for the Aztec word *coyotl,* which means "barking dog."

Coyotes are about the size of a medium German shepherd and are found in every state west of the Mississippi River. In spite of the loss of natural habitat due to the expansion of America's human population, the number of coyotes is on the increase. Their success is due primarily to their varied diet. A coyote will eat almost any small animal it can catch, including rodents, snakes, and insects. This omnivorous opportunist also eats berries, nuts, and food from garbage cans.

Many residents of the foothills and mountains have learned not to leave their small pets outside in their backyards at night. A hungry coyote just may be in the neighborhood looking for an easy meal!

Mile 41.9. Turn left into the parking area of the Mollie Kathleen Mine. If you wish to see Cripple Creek as the gold miners did, step onto the elevator of the Mollie Kathleen Mine. The cage elevator goes down 1,000 feet through a narrow shaft. When the

John Fielder

Scarlet Gilia

Scarlet gilia and skyrocket gilia are two of the most common names for this trumpet-shaped flower. The plant is about 12 to 15 inches tall. Oftentimes the tiny trumpets grow on just one side of the stalk, causing the plant to lean over with the weight of the flowers.

In the Pikes Peak region, the scarlet gilia is usually more pink or salmon in color than red. The wildflower thrives in sunny, dry locations and is very common along many of Colorado's roads and highways.

Above: Hikers find the perfect picnic spot at Mueller Ranch State Park.

John Fielder

Colorado's Columbine
A Stately Flower

The delicate, blue and white columbine is Colorado's state flower. It was chosen not only for its beauty, but also for the symbolism of its colors. The blue and white blossom stands for Colorado's blue skies and white snow; the gold center symbolizes the precious gold metal that Colorado is also famous for.

The columbine's common name comes from the Latin word *columba*, which means "dove." To many people, the white petals resemble dove wings.

Today, you can often find Colorado's state flower as you walk along mountain trails. Look for the columbine growing in moist, shady groves of aspen and evergreen trees.

elevator doors open, you are in a world of granite tunnels, stopes, drifts, and crosscuts. An experienced miner is your guide and he expertly navigates the labyrinth, explaining the difficult process of gold-mining, and pointing out rich gold veins threading through the granite rock. This is an adventurous way to begin your exploration of Cripple Creek and its history.

Turn left out of the parking area of the Mollie Kathleen Mine and drive down the hill to Cripple Creek.

Mile 43.4. Turn left into the parking area of the Cripple Creek and Victor Narrow Gauge Railroad. The open-air or glassed-in passenger

Below: Brick buildings from the 1890s still line Bennett Avenue in Cripple Creek.

Bill Bonebrake

Winfield Scott Stratton
Cripple Creek's First Millionaire

In Evergreen Cemetery, in Colorado Springs, the epitaph on Winfield Scott Stratton's gravestone reads, "It is not enough to help the feeble up, but to support him after." This epitaph reveals the philosophy of the millionaire miner of humble beginnings.

Born in Indiana in 1848, Stratton learned drafting and carpentry from his father, who was a boat builder. When Stratton moved to Colorado Springs in 1871, he made his living as a carpenter and contractor. As often as possible, he prospected for gold in the nearby mountains and studied geology and metallurgy.

After 17 years of prospecting, he made an educated guess and staked two claims in Cripple Creek, naming them the Independence and the Washington. In 1893, after two more years of working his claims, he struck a huge vein of gold, and immediately became famous as the gold district's first millionaire.

Stratton made an average of $1 million every year until he sold his claims in 1899 for $10 million. He had become a very wealthy man. However, instead of spending the money on material possessions for himself, Stratton began to finance projects that helped working families and the down-and-out.

In Cripple Creek, Stratton recruited unemployed miners and put them to work. When the town was devastated by a fire in 1896, Stratton came to the rescue. The moment he heard about the tragedy, he arranged and paid for a special train to be loaded with food, blankets, tents, and even baby diapers. The relief train arrived in Cripple Creek just a few hours after the fire.

In Colorado Springs, Stratton distributed winter coal to many households, paid for free concerts in the park, and built a trolley car system where everyone could travel its entire 41-mile route for only five cents a day. He also bought 2,400 acres to establish a home for the elderly and children in need. Named after his father, the Myron Stratton Home was created to look like a college campus with curving roads, beautiful buildings, shaded lawns, and unobstructed views of Cheyenne Mountain.

Today, a century later, Winfield Scott Stratton is remembered more for the money he gave away than for the amount of money he made.

Colorado Springs Pioneers Museum

cars of this narrow-gauge train provide grand views of mines, mountains, and aspen trees. The 45-minute ride, narrated by the train engineer, takes you past old mines and ghost towns. Try to imagine 500 working mines and three separate railroad lines connecting the mining district north to Divide, east to Colorado Springs, and south to the Cañon City area.

John Fielder

Aspen Trees

In Cripple Creek, visitors strike it rich each autumn when the hillsides fill with gold—the shimmering, golden leaves of aspen trees. One of Colorado's favorite trees, the aspen is probably the most photographed in every season of the year. In spring, aspen groves add a velvety sheen of green to the mountainsides. In summer, their bright green leaves are striking against the clear, blue sky. And in winter, the aspen's straight, white trunks cast pale shadows on the snow-covered mountain slopes.

Aspen trunks are often scarred—evidence of deer and elk feeding on, or scraping their antlers against, the soft bark.

After the train ride, take some time to see the Cripple Creek Museum, which is adjacent to the train station. This three-story building was the 1895 train depot of the Midland Terminal Railroad. Today it features exhibits of gold ore, mining equipment, railroad maps and photographs, a huge three-dimensional model of Cripple Creek's underground mining tunnels, and Victorian period clothing and furniture.

Most people also enjoy a stroll along Bennett Avenue, Cripple Creek's main street. Many gambling casinos are now housed in the late 1890s brick buildings lining the avenue.

Reset your odometer to zero when you leave the railroad parking area for your return to Colorado Springs. Retrace your drive back toward the town of Divide on Highway 67.

Mile 14.4. Turn left into the entrance of Mueller Ranch State Park. Be prepared to stop and pay the park entry fee. Maps are also available at the park gate.

Mile 16.0. Turn left into the parking lot of the Mueller Ranch Visitor Center. One of Colorado's newest state parks, Mueller Ranch State Park contains more than 12,000 acres of forests and meadows that serve as habitat for many native animals, including elk, deer, bighorn sheep, and black bear. The park is laced with hiking trails and staff is available to help visitors find the perfect hike, picnic spot, or camping area.

Turn right when you leave the Visitor Center parking lot, and retrace your drive back to Highway 67.

Reset your odometer to zero when you reach Highway 67.

Turn left onto Highway 67 and drive north to Divide.

Mile 3.9. Turn right onto Highway 24 and return to Colorado Springs.

Mile 28.9. The tour ends at the intersection of Interstate 25 and Highway 24, where your trip to gold country began.

5 Florissant Fossil Beds/ Manitou Lake

The Ute Trail was established by American Indians uncounted generations ago. In historic times, the Ute traveled the trail between seasonal hunting grounds.

Later, New World Spaniards used this pathway that led from the Great Plains into the Rocky Mountains, and eventually explorers for the United States government, pioneers, and miners also traversed Ute Trail.

Highway 24 traces Ute Trail as it leads up and over Ute Pass. This tour takes you over the ancient trail to a place of even older lakes and giant redwood trees. At Florissant Fossil Beds National Monument, you will find huge petrified tree trunks that thrived over 30 million years ago interspersed among today's ponderosa pine trees.

After leaving the remnants of Lake Florissant, stroll along the shore of thriving Lake Manitou before returning to Colorado Springs.

Ute Pass to Florissant Fossil Beds National Monument and Manitou Lake Tour

Total Mileage of Tour: 87.2 miles

Mile 0.0. Set your odometer to zero at the intersection of Interstate 25 and Highway 24 in Colorado Springs. This is Interstate Exit 141. Head west on Highway 24 as it leads into the mountains.

Winding up mountainous Ute Pass, you will pass the communities of Cascade, Chipita Park, Green Mountain Falls, and Crystola, which were all established in the late 1800s. The names of these small communities evoke images of mountain havens and, for the most part, they were established for just that reason—to be summer places for extended vacations.

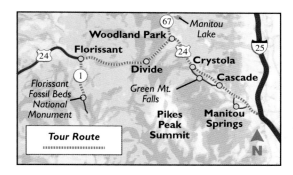

These small towns each built resort hotels with balconies and romantic names, such as The Ramona. The Colorado Midland Railroad brought summer vacationers and families on Sunday afternoon outings to the mountain towns. The resorts thrived from the 1890s until the 1920s.

The small communities each retain their charm and identity today. The many year-round residents note the arrival of June when vacationers return to their summer cabins in the mountains. Some of the vacation cottages have been in the same family for three to four generations.

Winston Walker

The American Elk

Bull elk, with huge racks of antlers and heads held high, move through the forests and meadows in a stately manner. The Division of Wildlife estimates that 2,000 elk make up the Pikes Peak herd.

Visitors and newcomers to Colorado are sometimes uncertain how to tell elk apart from deer. The most obvious differences can be observed in their size and in the shape of their antlers.

Elk are much larger than deer. A mature bull elk stands 5 feet at the shoulder and weighs up to 1,000 pounds. A mule deer buck measures just over 3 feet at the shoulder and weighs up to 400 pounds.

Additionally, an elk's antlers sweep back away from the head and are positioned above the shoulders. Each antler branches along one main beam. Conversely, the mule deer's antlers curve up and forward, framing the deer's ears, and branch two or three times.

Look for both of these large mammals whenever you are driving in the mountains.

Bob Toepfer

Above: Calm waters of Manitou Lake reflect Pikes Peak's north face.

Mile 15.0. Continue on Highway 24 through the towns of Woodland Park and Divide. Ute Pass reaches its highest elevation at 9,165 feet in Divide.

Mile 33.5. Turn left at the small town of Florissant onto Highway 1. Florissant, which means flowering in French, was named by Frank Castello, who settled here in the 1870s. He named his new home after his former town of Florissant, Missouri, and after the profusion of summer wildflowers.

Mile 36.0. Turn right into the entrance and parking lot of Florissant Fossil Beds National Monument. Florissant Fossil Beds is an ancient lake bed. Beginning about 35 million years ago, a long period of volcanic activity changed the landscape near Lake Florissant. Volcanic mudflows encased the redwood forests at the lake's edge. Over the years, repeated volcanic ashfalls trapped millions of insects and leaves. The small animals and leaves sank to the lake bottom, were covered over by sediments, and eventually became fossils.

Today, Florissant Fossil Beds National Monument is internationally famous among paleontologists for its astounding yield of insect and plant fossils. More than 60,000 individual fossils have been found, and more are found each year as research continues.

Although the huge trunks of the petrified redwood trees are very conspicuous, it is the tiny fossils that have most opened the window to the world of 35 million years ago.

The national monument's Visitor Center offers exhibits, guided walks and programs, a bookstore, and restrooms. Like all national parks and monuments,

Below: Cattails and marsh grasses display fall colors on the edge of Manitou Lake.

Weldon Lee

Abert's Squirrel

If you think you've seen a rabbit that climbs trees, then you have seen an Abert's squirrel. Long tufts of fur on this squirrel's ears cause it to resemble a rabbit, especially from a distance.

Also known as the tassel-eared squirrel, the Abert's squirrel is usually black or dark brown in color. It lives only in the ponderosa pine forests of Colorado, Utah, Arizona, and New Mexico. It builds its nest high in the pines for protection from predators and eats the ponderosa's pine cones, the inner bark of its twigs, and its soft new buds.

Look for this unusual looking squirrel as you walk through the ponderosa forests at Florissant Fossil Beds National Monument.

Colorado Springs Pioneers Museum

Florissant Fossil Beds has excellent self-guided materials, including trail, wildflower, and bird guides.

If your time permits, take both self-guided hikes. The Walk Through Time loop trail is only one-half mile and circles through the ponderosa forest. The one-mile Petrified Forest loop trail leads through forest and meadow with a stop by a giant petrified

Buckskin Charlie
Chief of the Southern Ute

In 1840, the year Buckskin Charlie was born, the Ute homeland stretched from the eastern plains of present-day Colorado, west across the high peaks and plateaus, and into the mountains and canyons of eastern Utah and northern New Mexico. The oral history of the Ute proclaims that this region has always been their homeland; archaeologists concur that the Ute are the oldest continuous residents of Colorado.

Buckskin Charlie was born near the Garden of the Gods and was a member of the Capote band, one of the seven bands that made up the Ute People in historical times. The Ute had been in contact with Western Europeans since the early 1600s when the Spaniards were exploring their land claims in North America and trading with the various American Indians of the Southwest that they met.

This initial contact with the Spanish changed the lives of the Ute People. From the Spaniards, the Ute obtained the horse. Then, instead of living primarily on the bounty of the mountains—the elk, deer, small animals, and many edible plants—the Ute began to travel much farther on horseback to hunt buffalo. This brought them into contact and conflict with the Cheyenne, Arapaho, Kiowa, Sioux, and Comanche—American Indians of the Great Plains.

The next period of unfathomable change for the Ute began soon after 1860. Thousands of settlers and miners moved into the Colorado Territory with the discovery of gold and the building of railroads, causing inevitable conflicts between the Ute and the newcomers.

Buckskin Charlie became chief of the Southern Ute in 1880, following the death of Chief Ouray, and he led his people during this time of tumultuous change. Like his predecessor, Buckskin Charlie realized that fighting the newcomers would be futile. Instead, over a period of years, Chief Ouray, then Buckskin Charlie and the Ute Elders were able to negotiate with the United States government to retain a portion of their traditional homeland for their reservation rather than to be relocated. The seven bands of the Ute People went to live on three separate reservations—the Southern Ute and Ute Mountain reservations in southwestern Colorado, and the Uintah Ouray Reservation in northeastern Utah.

Buckskin Charlie, pictured with his wife Emma Naylor Buck, is credited with leading the Southern Ute in adapting to life on the reservation while keeping alive their traditional ceremonies, religion, festivals, and language. When Buckskin Charlie died in 1936 at the age of 96, he had lived to see the Ute regain their strength. Along with all other American Indians, the Ute People became United States citizens in 1924.

Today, the Ute are part of the rich cultural fabric of Colorado. Although the reservations remain a focal point, the Ute live throughout the state, contributing their knowledge of the land, and excelling in the arts, education, and business.

redwood trunk that is 38 feet in circumference. The brochures for the self-guided trails are available at the Visitor Center information desk. Both trails are wide and graveled, fairly level, and are designated as wheelchair accessible.

Shaded picnic facilities are located near the parking lot. As you leave Florissant Fossil Beds, notice the unusual weather vane on top of the old barn across from the National Monument's entrance.

Turn left out of the parking lot and return to Highway 24.

Reset your odometer to 0.0 when you return to Highway 24.

Turn right on Highway 24 and head back to Woodland Park.

Mile 14.8. Turn left in Woodland Park at the stoplight for Highway 67. Woodland Park was established in 1890 and named Manitou Park. However, the founders of Manitou Springs, fearing confusion over the two Manitou names, persuaded the new town to change its name. The new name better suited the town. It soon became

Redwood Tree Fossils

The largest fossil tree stump at Florissant Fossil Beds is 38 feet in circumference and 12 feet tall. It is estimated that it was 700 years old and more than 200 feet tall—about three times taller than today's big ponderosas nearby—when volcanic mudflows surged around it. The tree became petrified when minerals slowly replaced the woody tissues and hardened, turning the tree into rock.

The petrified tree stumps at Florissant Fossil Beds are clues to this region's ancient climate and geology. The tree fossils are of extinct giant sequoias, or redwood trees. Their relatives today grow along the coast of California, where the climate is much wetter than in Colorado. Did this region receive much more rain 35 million years ago?

The trees were preserved in a volcanic mudflow when volcanoes were active millions of years ago. Now, volcanic activity has ceased. Will it resume? Fossils are clues and puzzle pieces to the past. Research continues at Florissant Fossil Beds in hopes of answering questions regarding the past, and to anticipate the future.

a source of lumber and railroad ties for Colorado's fast-growing towns and railroads. At one point, the pine forests surrounding Woodland Park supported five sawmills.

Mile 22.2. Turn right into the entrance and parking areas of Manitou Lake. Expect to pay a small fee.

Manitou Lake is a great place to spend an afternoon or a whole day. Its blue water reflects a stunning view of Pikes Peak's north face, and wildlife abounds. Many shaded picnic tables are

The Ponderosa Pine

The ponderosa's spreading, ungainly-shaped branches make it easy to identify from a distance. Its pine needles are 7 inches long and, upon close inspection, its tree bark looks like jigsaw-puzzle pieces. The ponderosa pine cones are a source of food for birds and other wildlife.

Drought-tolerant and fire-resistant, the ponderosa is well-suited to the dry soils and climate of the Pikes Peak region.

located on the lake's forested west side, and a wheelchair-accessible boardwalk traverses the cattail wetlands of the lake's south shore.

Other activities at Manitou Lake include fishing, bicycling the 12-mile round-trip bicycle trail that parallels Highway 67, and wildlife watching. The meadows on the lake's east side are filled with wildflowers in the summer.

Reset your odometer to 0.0 when you leave the parking lot and **turn left** onto Highway 67 to return to Woodland Park.

Mile 7.4. Turn left onto Highway 24 and return to Colorado Springs. It is 15.5 miles back to the intersection of Highway 24 and Interstate 25 where this tour began. Enjoy the foothills views as you head down Ute Pass.

6 Cañon City/Royal Gorge

Cañon City, which uses the Spanish spelling of canyon, is definitely well named. In the mid-1600s, Spanish missionaries exploring north from New Mexico told of the deep chasm in the Arkansas River where the mountains meet the plains. The 1,000-foot-deep "Grand Canyon of the Arkansas River" is carved through almost solid granite.

The low hills and canyon country to the north of Cañon City also hold surprises. This region contains the Morrison rock formation, which yields 150-million-year-old fossils from the Jurassic period. Paleontologists have been working in this area for over 100 years and have discovered more than 25 different kinds of dinosaurs. The Dinosaur Depot in Cañon City exhibits some of the discoveries from this historic dig location.

Cañon City's Dinosaur Depot and the Royal Gorge Tour

Total Mileage of Tour: 120 *miles round-trip*

Mile 0.0. Set your odometer to zero at the intersection of Interstate 25 and Highway 115, Interstate Exit 140. Drive south on Highway 115 away from downtown Colorado Springs.

Mile 3.0. On the right, Cheyenne Mountain, at 9,565 feet, is the most prominent mountain of the foothills. It is named for the Cheyenne American Indians. On the left is the Fort Carson Army Base, named after Kit Carson, the famous 1800s mountain man and guide.

Mile 10.8. The highway curves through red rocks that are part of the same geologic formation as Garden of the Gods Park.

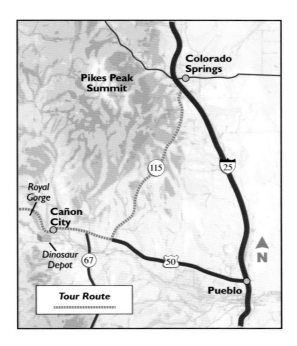

Mile 13.2. The Sangre de Cristo mountain range can be seen to the southwest for most of the remaining drive to Cañon City. This lofty range has 13 peaks over 14,000 feet high. Its Spanish name means "blood of Christ." When the sun strikes these snow-capped peaks at dawn, the entire mountain range turns crimson.

Opposite: A life-size Allosaurus model seems to pursue unsuspecting visitors at the Dinosaur Depot.

Mile 15.3. The Turkey Creek Ranch once belonged to Broadmoor Hotel owners Spencer and Julie Penrose, who raised horses and had a Spanish-style ranch home near the creek. Today, their ranch is part of Fort Carson.

Piñon pines and juniper trees that make up the forest of the Southwest cover the low hills along the highway from here to the Royal Gorge.

Mile 33.1. Turn right at the intersection of Highway 115 and Highway 50, and continue driving west on Highway 50.

Mile 37.6. Note that this turnoff to Cripple Creek is not a shortcut. It is a very narrow, winding road, and subject to washouts.

Cañon City lies in Fremont County, named after John Charles Fremont, who led five expeditions in the 1840s and 1850s into what is now Colorado. He camped in the Cañon City area and explored the Arkansas River. Later, he became the first governor of California.

Mile 41.8. On the right is the Cañon City Visitor Information Center; it is open during the summer months.

The town of Cañon City was settled in 1860 by Anson Rudd, a blacksmith who became the first warden of the Colorado Territorial Prison. His original 1860 log cabin has been preserved and is part of the Cañon City Municipal Museum at 612 Royal Gorge Boulevard.

Note that within the city limits, Highway 50 is named Royal Gorge Boulevard.

Weldon Lee

Mile 44.6. Turn left onto 4th Street. You can't miss the Dinosaur Depot on the corner of 4th Street and Royal Gorge Boulevard. Park either on 4th Street or in the convenient parking lot behind the Depot.

The Dinosaur Depot is a great place to learn about dinosaurs. Unlike a very large museum, visitors aren't overwhelmed, and can enjoy several hands-on exhibits, including dinosaur eggs and a Stegosaurus spike.

The highlight of a visit to the Depot is the chance to see pale-ontologists at work on the Stegosaurus fossil that was discovered

The Mountain Lion
An Animal Built for Action

Mountain lions have many common names, including cougar and catamount. This large American cat is a solitary predator and hunts mostly at dawn and dusk. It quietly stalks its preferred prey—the mule deer. The home range of a mountain lion can vary from as little as 10 square miles to a vast area encompassing 370 square miles.

Full-grown male lions are over 8 feet long from nose to tail and can weigh more than 200 pounds. Their padded tracks are similar in shape to a house cat's paw print, but in size, the large 4-inch-wide tracks are disturbing and instantly command respect.

In spite of their large size, mountain lions are able to leap 40 feet, jump 18 feet straight up, run faster than a deer, and easily climb trees. This powerful predator thrives in the foothills surrounding Pikes Peak wherever mule deer are plentiful.

north of Cañon City in 1992. A glassed-in laboratory gives visitors a look at a rare sight—a 150-million-year-old Stegosaurus.

The museum also features an outdoor plaza with dinosaur tracks and a life-size Allosaurus. A media presentation, and a chance to ask questions of staff and volunteers, round out a fun visit to this small museum with its big fossils.

The Dinosaur Depot is operated by the Garden Park Paleontology Society in cooperation with the City of Cañon City, the Bureau of Land Management, and the Denver Museum of Natural History.

Return to Royal Gorge Boulevard and continue west toward the Royal Gorge.

Mile 52.6. Turn left off Highway 50 at the Royal Gorge entrance sign. The entrance road winds for 4.3 miles through the piñon pine and juniper forest.

Mile 56.9. The Royal Gorge is an unusual combination of a National Natural Landmark and an amusement park. The Royal

Denver Public Library

Othniel Charles Marsh
Pioneer Paleontologist

In the 1800s, paleontology—the study of ancient life—was a new scientific field. The word "dinosaur" was coined in the 1840s, and only about 10 dinosaurs had been found.

This situation changed rapidly in the 1870s when two very successful and competitive paleontologists became rivals. Othniel Charles Marsh of Yale and Edward D. Cope of the University of Pennsylvania raced to see whose fossil-finding teams could discover the most new dinosaurs. Their long-running feud over fossils was eventually labeled the "Bone Wars."

Both men quarried in the Cañon City Garden Park Fossil Area of Colorado and in other western states, and made very important discoveries. By the end of their careers, more than 136 different dinosaurs had been discovered and named.

The most famous finds in the Cañon City area from Marsh's quarries included the Diplodocus, the Stegosaurus, and the Allosaurus. These fossils were sent to the Smithsonian Museum in Washington, D.C., and have been part of their collection for more than 100 years.

Scientists still discover dinosaur fossils in the rock formations north of Cañon City, following the lead of the legendary 19th century paleontologists.

Gorge Bridge is privately owned and the entry fee covers all the rides in the park—from an aerial tramway over the gorge, to the incline railway to the bottom of the canyon, to a children's carousel and other rides.

A highlight is walking across the highest suspension bridge in the world, but it is not recommended for anyone who has acrophobia!

Even with all the activity of the rides on its rim, the Royal Gorge itself is still the main attraction. The chasm is 1,053 feet deep—so deep that you can barely hear the Arkansas River rushing at the bottom of the gorge.

Like the Colorado River at the Grand Canyon, the Arkansas River cut the Royal Gorge over millions of

Stegosaurus Dinosaur Discovery

Colorado school students led the effort in 1987 to have the Stegosaurus named Colorado's official state fossil. After all, the first Stegosaurus fossil ever discovered in the world was found in Colorado, just west of Denver.

This plant-eating dinosaur was about 10 feet tall, 24 feet long, and weighed 2 tons. For protection from predators, the Stegosaurus had four sharp tail-spikes pointing outward horizontally from the end of its tail (two spikes on each side), and 18 to 20 bony plates attached to its backbone. The big plates, some up to 3 feet high, may have also helped the Stegosaurus to cool down on hot days— similar to a radiator.

In 1992, paleontologists from the Denver Museum of Natural History discovered a Stegosaurus fossil in the foothills north of Cañon City in the Garden Park Fossil Area. This nearly complete dinosaur skeleton showed conclusively, for the first time, the exact position of the Stegosaurus's tail spikes (shown near the paleontologist's elbow in the photo). The 12-inch spikes are attached to and project outward from the sides of the tail, rather than upward as earlier thought.

To better study the 150-million-year-old Stegosaurus, 6 tons of rock encasing the fossil were carefully airlifted by helicopter from the paleontology dig site to a waiting semitrailer, then trucked to the museum. The Stegosaurus, on loan from the Denver Museum of Natural History, is exhibited at Cañon City's Dinosaur Depot where it continues to be painstakingly excavated.

Garden Park Paleontology Society

years. As the mountains slowly rose, the river continued cutting away at the rocks. Given time, western rivers have a lot to show for their incessant movement.

Retrace the road back to Highway 50.

Reset your odometer to 0.0 when you turn right (east) onto Highway 50.

Mile 7.7. Note the shaded city park on the right that is a great location for a picnic. In addition to picnic tables and restrooms, it has a visitor information booth during the summer months.

Mile 19.3. Exit right off Highway 50, then turn left onto Highway 115 for the 33-mile drive back to Colorado Springs. When you reach Interstate 25, you are back where you started and have completed this tour of Cañon City country.

Above: The Royal Gorge Bridge spans the 1,000-foot chasm carved by the Arkansas River.

Weldon Lee

The Black-Billed Magpie
An Adaptable and Intelligent Bird

Magpies are known for their ability to adapt to situations that enhance their ability to survive. Historically, magpies in North America followed the huge buffalo herds, eating insects stirred up in the dust and on the buffaloes' backs. Even today, magpies eat insects on the backs of elk, mule deer, and bighorn sheep, and in winter they have been known to find warmth by roosting on the backs of cattle.

Magpies live in small flocks and communicate with family members through a variety of musical whistles and raucous calls. When the magpie was once kept as a pet, it was capable of mimicking human speech.

Nest-building is a big event for magpies. In spring, the female magpie builds a large, dome-shaped nest from sticks that the male brings to her. The nest is built to last, and reaches 2 to 4 feet high with a side entrance. After the nesting season, other birds sometimes take shelter from wind and rain in the magpie's abandoned nest.

The slow-flying, black and white magpies and their dome-shaped nests are familiar sights in the Pikes Peak region throughout the year.

Pueblo/ Arkansas River

A river can be a landmark, a pathway, a boundary, or a meeting place. The Arkansas River is all of these.

For centuries, the Arkansas was a landmark and a pathway for the American Indians who lived along its banks and tributaries. When Spaniards began traveling northward from New Mexico in the early 1600s, the Arkansas was plotted on their maps as the El Rio Grande de San Francisco and became their landmark and pathway.

In 1806, Zebulon Pike's expedition followed the Arkansas, as did the 1820 Stephen Long expedition. They explored stretches of the Arkansas River and its tributaries and mapped the information for the United States.

Before the Louisiana Purchase in 1803, the Arkansas River marked the international boundary between French and Spanish territory. After the Purchase and until the mid-1800s, it was the dividing line between United States territory and Mexico.

The Arkansas was a meeting place in 1842 when five trappers from Taos, New Mexico, constructed a small adobe fort at the confluence of the Arkansas River and Fountain Creek. The fort was named El Pueblo and was used mainly as a trading post. Although El Pueblo was abandoned after a few years, the town of Pueblo was organized just a few years later in 1860 in the same location.

The city of Pueblo, with its Arkansas River, is one of the best places in the state to explore the cultural roots of Colorado.

Pueblo and the Arkansas River Tour

Total Mileage of Tour: 94.5 *miles*

Mile 0.0. Set your odometer to zero at the intersection of Interstate 25 and Highway 24, Interstate Exit 141. Drive south on Interstate 25. The city of Pueblo is 40 miles south of Colorado Springs. As you drive toward Pueblo, on the left (east) side of the interstate, you will see Fountain Creek lined by cottonwood trees. The river-sized creek flows into the Arkansas River at Pueblo.

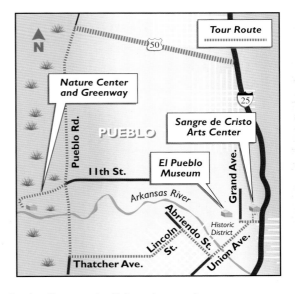

Mile 31.5. Look to the south. The two mountains known as the Spanish Peaks dominate the southern horizon. The higher of the two peaks is 13,623 feet tall.

Mile 42.0. Exit off the interstate at Exit 98-B onto 1st Street. As you exit, the Sangre de Cristo Arts and Conference Center is in view on your right.

Turn right onto Santa Fe Avenue, and then right into the parking lot of the Arts Center.

The terraced, shaded courtyards and intricate patterns of tiles provide a beautiful entry to the Arts Center's galleries. The Arts Center is known for its permanent collection of western art, for its

Opposite:
Pueblo's south-
western heritage
is evident in the
architecture
of the Pueblo
Greenway and
Nature Center.

musical and theatrical productions, and for its appealing architecture. An excellent children's museum is also located at the Arts Center, offering interactive activities for the younger set.

Turn left onto Santa Fe Avenue when you leave the Arts Center, then turn right at the stoplight onto 1st Street. Drive three blocks to the El Pueblo Museum. Metered parking is available on the street. You may also choose to walk to the museum from the Arts Center.

The Museum is built on the site of the 1842 El Pueblo Trading Post. Part of the excitement of this museum is that the old trading post is still being excavated by archaeologists and may

Below:
Intricate tiles
decorate the
terrace of the
Sangre de
Cristo Arts and
Conference
Center.

*Above:
Cottonwoods
shade walkers
along the
Arkansas
River Trail.*

reveal additional information and artifacts about the region's past. The Museum chronicles the history of this part of southern Colorado, including the separate and intertwining histories of the American Indians and the Hispanic and Anglo explorers and settlers. A walk-in teepee, a southern Colorado time line, many historical photographs, and Pueblo's more recent history are also portrayed.

Drive east (back toward the interstate) on 1st Street for one block when you leave the Museum. Turn right (south) onto Union Street.

Reset your odometer to zero at the intersection of 1st Street and Union Street.

John Fielder

Prickly Pear Cactus

Cacti are unusual plants. Without green leaves, they carry out photosynthesis in their fleshy, green stems. The prickly pear cactus has a waxy, tough outer covering that helps it retain moisture—an essential feature for its survival in dry conditions.

The prickly pear cactus grows close to the ground and is a relative of the cholla, or candelabra, cactus that branches upright like a tree. Both are common in southern Colorado.

Charles Goodnight
A Real Cowboy

If you like to read western novels or watch old western movies, you have probably heard of the Goodnight-Loving Trail. In the 1870s, Charles Goodnight and his partner, Oliver Loving, blazed a cattle trail 2,000 miles long from Texas to Wyoming, driving their longhorn cattle over millions of acres of open range land. It is estimated that 8,000 to 10,000 head of cattle made up the huge drives.

The Goodnight-Loving Trail began in Texas and headed west into New Mexico. Then the cattle trail turned north and climbed over Raton Pass to the Colorado Territory, crossed the Arkansas River near Pueblo, and finally ended near Denver. Some cattle were driven even farther north to the Wyoming area. Although the cattle drives were long and dangerous, they were profitable at the end of the trail. In the supply towns for the mountain mining camps, a steer sold for $60 instead of the $10 going rate in Texas.

During this time, Charles Goodnight's ranch near Pueblo served as the headquarters for the long cattle drives. Today, the ranch's stone barn still stands as a reminder of the "Old West." When the cattle driving days came to an end, Goodnight left his Pueblo ranch and moved to the Texas Panhandle.

Even though the cattle drives lasted only nine years, the cowboys and their cattle trail adventures are legendary in American popular culture. Today, Charles Goodnight and his "home on the range" life are remembered in the National Cowboy Hall of Fame Museum in Oklahoma City, Oklahoma.

Mile 0.2. Note the old brick buildings of Pueblo's old town, the Union Avenue Historic District. Most of the brick and stone buildings lining the avenue were built in the 1880s when the town of Pueblo began to thrive. Both the Denver and Rio Grande and the Santa Fe Railroads linked Pueblo to the state and the nation's rail system, and in 1881, the Colorado Fuel and Iron Company (CF&I) was founded. CF&I grew to be the biggest steel maker in the West by 1900. It supplied steel rails for the expanding western railroad systems and barbed wire for the fences rapidly being erected throughout the West.

John Bates

Today the Union Avenue Historic District is lined with specialty shops and restaurants. Adjacent to Union Avenue, a multimillion-dollar riverwalk is being constructed that will be an oasis for everyone downtown to enjoy.

Mile 0.5. Look to the right as you drive over the Arkansas River. The huge mural decorating the floodway is more than 3 miles long and is listed in the *Guinness Book of World Records* as the longest mural in the world. Begun unofficially in 1979, the mural is now a collaborative, ongoing community project.

Plains Yucca

In mid- to late June, tall stalks of creamy plains yucca flowers cover many hills and mesas in the Pikes Peak region. The pale blossoms attract night-flying moths that pollinate the yucca. Then, within a few weeks, the flowers become bulky, 2- to 4-inch seedpods. The yucca seeds are a good source of food for wildlife. Even after a deep snowfall, birds can fly to the tall yucca stalks and feast on the seeds.

American Indians of the Southwest traditionally have used every part of the yucca. The long, tough leaves were woven into baskets and the strong, stringy leaf fibers were used to make twine and rope. The yucca's flower petals are edible, and its taproot is used to make soap—the reason for its other common name, "soapweed."

The yucca is very common in the open prairies surrounding Pueblo and bordering the Pikes Peak foothills.

Mile 0.8. Turn right onto Abriendo Street.

Mile 1.5. Turn left onto Lincoln Street, which becomes Thatcher Street.

Mile 2.8. As you drive through Pueblo's municipal golf course, imagine a time in the 1870s when Charles Goodnight was driving cattle. The golf course area was part of Goodnight's ranch, where longhorn cattle grazed on prairie grasses.

Mile 3.5. Turn right onto Pueblo Boulevard.

Weldon Lee

The Great Horned Owl
Efficient in Total Darkness

If you listen intently on a cold winter's night in January, you just may hear the Whoo! Whoo-whoo-whoo! Whoo! Whoo! call of a great horned owl. The call heralds the beginning of the owl's breeding season, as the male and female call to each other and establish a nesting site. In early February, the female lays her eggs, and the owlets hatch about 30 days later, possibly during a March snowstorm!

The male and female take turns incubating the eggs, and when the eggs hatch, the male brings food to its mate and the fast-growing owlets.

The great horned owl is a nocturnal bird of prey, hunting its prey of mice, birds, rabbits, and other small animals throughout the night. The owl is well equipped to successfully locate and kill its prey in total darkness.

Although owls have good night vision, they depend even more on their acute hearing. The feathers that surround an owl's eyes and face form "facial disks" that capture and funnel sound waves into the owl's ear openings. Relying solely upon its sense of hearing, an owl can locate and seize a tiny mouse in its talons, without the aid of even the dimmest starlight.

Mile 4.8. Turn left onto 11th Street.

Mile 5.6. Note the Raptor Center on the left. This is a recommended stop when you return from the Arkansas River.

Mile 5.8. Stop and park at the Pueblo Greenway and Nature Center, also the location of the Café del Río Restaurant and a major access point for the Arkansas River Trail. The tall cottonwood trees almost hide one of southern Colorado's best recreation areas. A walk or bicycle ride along the shady, paved riverside trail is a favorite activity for both locals and out-of-town visitors. Bird watchers can look for orioles and kingfishers, and children can enjoy the large playground.

Exploring the Nature Center, picnicking, fishing, river rafting, and dining at the sidewalk cafe are all possible at this location along the Arkansas River.

Weldon Lee

The Great Blue Heron

Great blue herons seem almost out of place in land-locked Colorado. Their spindly legs are obviously suited to wading in water; their curved necks and long beaks are adapted to catching fish.

Yet, Colorado's large river systems, lakes, and reservoirs provide ample habitat for herons. The large, 4-foot-tall birds eat primarily other animals that are found in and near water. Small fish, frogs, garter snakes, water insects, and crayfish are their main diet.

Herons build their nests in the top branches of cottonwood trees and usually return to the same trees every spring. Look for a heronry—a group of nesting herons—as you explore the Arkansas River area in late spring or summer.

Retrace your route on 11th Street after leaving the Nature Center.

Mile 6.1. Turn right into the parking area of the Pueblo Raptor Center. Injured birds of prey, such as golden eagles, bald eagles, hawks, and owls, are rehabilitated at this unique facility and then set free. At the Raptor Center, you can get an up-close look at these beautiful birds and learn more about them and other wildlife from this part of the state.

Mile 6.9. Turn left onto Pueblo Boulevard.

Mile 9.4. Turn right onto Highway 50 and drive east to meet the interstate.

Mile 12.2. Turn left onto Interstate 25 and drive north back to Colorado Springs.

Mile 52.0. When you return to Interstate Exit 141, you are back where you started, at the intersection of Interstate 25 and Highway 24 in Colorado Springs.

8 Downtown Colorado Springs

In 1869 when General William Jackson Palmer first conceived the idea to build a beautiful city near the confluence of Monument and Fountain Creeks, the location was all potential. It had great views and wide-open spaces, but no railroad, no navigable river, no established marketable resource, and no trees. Nevertheless, Palmer set to work.

With the support of wealthy investors from the eastern United States and from England, and the loyalty of friends from his Civil War days, Palmer began to plan his city. Even before his new town site had been surveyed, he started building a railroad south from Denver to connect with Fountain Colony—his first choice of names for the new town.

In 1871, Palmer and his surveyors settled on the name Colorado Springs, and platted the city of his dreams with wide streets and avenues, places for parks, churches, and a college. Palmer directed the planting of thousands of trees, built the first hotel, brought railroad transportation and commerce to town, and advertised Colorado Springs extensively throughout the United States and England as a vacation and health resort.

In the 1890s when gold was discovered in Cripple Creek, Colorado Springs also struck it rich. New millionaires invested in thriving Colorado Springs and built their mansions along the wide avenues. Cripple Creek fortunes funded opera houses, trolley car systems, more parks, hotels, railroads, banks, schools, and churches. Before the close of the 19th century, Colorado Springs had become the place that Palmer had envisioned and described in a letter in 1869, "where the air is fraught with health and vigor, and where life would be poetry."

Downtown Colorado Springs and Monument Valley Park Tour

Total Mileage of Tour: 5.1 *miles*

All or any portion of this tour may also be walked. Tejon Street between Acacia Park and the Colorado Springs Pioneers Museum is a favorite walking and shopping area for local citizens. As you drive or walk downtown, note that the east-west streets, such as Boulder, St. Vrain, and Platte, are named for rivers and other locations that General Palmer scouted when looking for train routes for his narrow-gauge railroad. The north-south streets, such as Cascade and Nevada, are named for western mountain ranges.

Mile 0.0. Begin this tour at the intersection of Interstate 25 and Uintah Street, Interstate Exit 143. Drive east (away from the mountains) on Uintah Street until it intersects Cascade Avenue.

Mile 0.4. Turn right (south) onto Cascade Avenue. The Colorado College campus can be

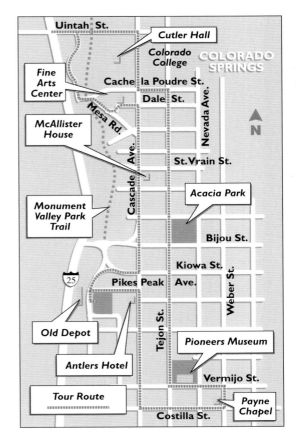

Weldon Lee

The Red Fox
A Better Mousetrap

The red fox lives throughout most of the United States and Canada and is quite common in Colorado Springs. It is often seen in broad daylight, running across a neighborhood street with its long, bushy tail streaming straight out.

This fox is fairly small, weighing only 10 to 15 pounds, and has thick reddish-orange fur, a bushy white-tipped tail, and black feet. Like coyotes, red foxes are omnivorous and eat rodents, ground-nesting birds, berries, and insects. However, mice are their main prey, and a grown male fox may eat up to 100 mice in one week!

Red foxes tend to live alone except during the spring breeding season. After the birth of the young, the male brings food to the female for several days as she stays in the den to nurse the pups. Soon, the fast-growing pups require the hunting skills of both parents to provide enough food. In midsummer, the parents begin to teach the young foxes how to hunt for themselves, and by fall, the young members of the fox family go their separate ways.

viewed on both sides of Cascade Avenue. The small college was established in 1874 by General Palmer, William Jackson (whose wife was Helen Hunt Jackson), Henry McAllister, Reverend Thomas Haskell, and others. General Palmer had included land for a "College Square" in his original 1871 town plat.

Mile 0.6. Look to the right to see Cutler Hall, the first permanent building of Colorado College. This handsome building

Opposite: Colorado College students take a break on the steps of Palmer Hall.

Colorado Springs Pioneers Museum

Alice Bemis Taylor
Arts Patron and Humanitarian

In Colorado Springs, people benefit daily from the legacy of Alice Bemis Taylor. Children are nurtured in the Colorado Springs Day Nursery, and students, residents, and visitors enjoy the arts, theater, and special events offered at the Fine Arts Center.

In 1881, Alice's father Judson Bemis moved his family from Massachusetts to Colorado with the hope that his wife's health would improve. Fortunately, the health of Mrs. Bemis did improve, and the Colorado Springs community began to benefit from the generosity of the wealthy new residents. Mr. Bemis donated a new residence hall to Colorado College, and Mrs. Bemis started the Colorado Springs Day Nursery for underprivileged children.

Alice grew up in Colorado Springs, and married Frederick Taylor in 1903. A few years later, they adopted a daughter named Doree. In 1923, Alice built a beautiful English-style mansion to house the Day Nursery that her mother had founded.

Alice was a member of the Colorado Springs Art Association and collected many southwestern works of art and artifacts, from Hispanic folk art to the textiles, basketry, pottery, and jewelry of the Navajo, Pueblo, and Jicarilla Apache. By the late 1920s, Alice had accumulated such an abundance of artwork that she began to plan a special museum to exhibit her collection.

With the assistance of two very influential women, Elizabeth Hare and Julie Penrose, Alice's plans became reality. By the time the Colorado Springs Fine Arts Center opened in 1936, Alice had donated almost $2 million for the construction and endowment of the new art center. The beautifully designed Fine Arts Center has grown from a regional treasure into a national asset with its historic and continuing acquisitions of southwestern art.

with its bell tower served the needs of the entire college when it was built in 1880. The hall was named for Henry Cutler, who donated money to the fledgling college as a favor to his close friend and first president of the college, Edward Tenney. Colorado College has thrived alongside Colorado Springs and today ranks as one of the best liberal arts colleges in the nation.

Mile 0.7. Turn left (east) onto Cache la Poudre Street and drive for one block.

Mile 0.8. Turn right (south) onto Tejon Street.

Mile 1.4. Look to the left to see Acacia Park. This park was established more than 125 years ago as part of Colorado Springs' original town plat. Today the shade trees, band shell with scheduled concerts in the summer, and children's playground make it an inviting oasis in the downtown area.

Mile 1.9. On the left is the Colorado Springs Pioneers Museum at 215 South Tejon Street. This is an excellent, free museum that highlights the region's cultural history. Metered parking is available either on Tejon Street or Vermijo Street.

The original 1903 building was the El Paso County Courthouse. It was constructed in the center of Alamo Park, one of the two park sites in General Palmer's 1871 town plat. The courthouse was converted into a museum in the early 1970s and has been restored to its original grandeur with interior columns, terrazzo floors, and decorated ceilings. Most visitors enjoy a ride in its antique elevator.

The old courthouse building functions well in its second role as a museum of the people. Permanent exhibits feature the Ute American Indians, General Palmer and his family, and Helen Hunt Jackson, and are complemented by a variety of traveling exhibits, such as quilt shows and depictions of the area's more recent history.

Mile 1.9. Turn left (east) on Vermijo Street.

Mile 2.1. Turn right (south) onto Weber Street. At the end of the block, at 320 South Weber, is one of the first church buildings constructed in Colorado Springs. The native stone church served the

The Plains Cottonwood

For the first inhabitants and travelers in this part of North America, the sight of cottonwood trees was like a neon sign advertising "Water!" Drinking water, shade, wood for a fire, and water for the travelers' animals were all available in a cottonwood grove.

Like the smaller aspen tree, the cottonwood is in the willow family and grows only where there is a river, stream, spring, or water near the surface of the ground. Also like the aspen, its heart-shaped leaves turn a brilliant golden color in the fall.

Tall cottonwoods provide essential habitat for a wide variety of birds, mammals, and other animals along Colorado's waterways. Yellow warblers look for insects among the cottonwood's top branches, an owl nests in a hollow in the tree's trunk, orioles hang their woven nests in the middle branches, a muskrat burrows under its roots in the bank of a stream, and a host of other animals make the cottonwood tree their home.

John Fielder

Colorado Springs Pioneers Museum

Reverend J. W. Braxton
Church Founder

In 1872, just one year after Colorado Springs was founded, Reverend J. W. Braxton held a church service in the home of Mr. and Mrs. Isaiah Carter. Mr. Carter's three brothers and their families also attended. This first church service was the beginning of the Payne Chapel African Methodist Episcopal (A.M.E.) Church, one of the oldest churches in Colorado Springs.

The dedicated new church members immediately sought to establish a permanent church building. Isaiah Carter contacted the Colorado Springs Company, headed by William Jackson Palmer, which was donating land to the city's handful of fledgling churches. Isaiah was successful in obtaining a choice lot, just one block southeast of Pioneer Square (today's Pioneers Museum location).

Within the first three years of the church's founding, Rev. Braxton and his faithful members built a frame building on their new land, and Payne Chapel A.M.E. began to thrive. The Chapel was named after Daniel Alexander Payne, a bishop of the African Methodist Episcopal Church.

From 1889 to 1891, the hard-working congregation built a beautiful stone church at their 128 Pueblo Avenue location. They convinced the U.S. Army Corps of Engineers to quarry and donate the sandstone from Bear Creek Canyon. Then, over a period of months, the church members loaded up their horse-drawn wagons and transported tons and tons of rock back to their church site where they constructed the entire building.

For almost 100 years, the Payne Chapel A.M.E. Church thrived at this downtown location. In the 1980s, when the congregation grew too big for the hand-built stone church, Payne Chapel relocated to a spacious new building a few miles to the northeast. At the new Payne Chapel, the tradition of faith and hard work, started by Reverend Braxton and the Carter families over 125 years ago, continues today.

congregation of the Payne Chapel African Methodist Episcopal Church in this location for more than 100 years. The congregation outgrew the beloved stone building in the 1980s and relocated northeast of downtown. The historic building has been converted to private office space.

Mile 2.2. Turn right (west) onto Costilla Street.

Mile 2.5. Turn right (north) onto Cascade Avenue.

Mile 2.9. The intersection of Cascade Avenue and Pikes Peak Avenue is where the first survey stake of the new town of Colorado Springs was driven on July 31, 1871.

To the right, next to Pikes Peak Avenue, a plaque commemorating the first stake is located just a few yards to the east of the sculpture of

William Jackson Palmer
Railroad Builder and City Founder

Colorado Springs Pioneers Museum

William Jackson Palmer accomplished so much during his lifetime that it seems he fit several lifetimes into one 72-year span. At Palmer Hall, in the center of the Colorado College campus, a huge bronze tablet honors Palmer with this summation of his achievements:

> Union Cavalry General, pioneer railroad builder, prophet of Colorado's greatness. He mapped the routes of three transcontinental railways, supervised the building of the first [rail]road to Denver, organized and constructed the Denver and Rio Grande Railroad, stimulated the State's industries, cherished its beauties, founded Colorado Springs, fostered Colorado College, and served our Sister Republic of Mexico with sympathy and wisdom in developing its national railways.

The tablet is just one of five bronze memorials throughout the United States and Mexico to William Jackson Palmer. The locations of the other four tablets partially tell the story of Palmer's unforgettable accomplishments.

At the Hampton Institute in Virginia, Palmer is noted for his generosity in funding the buildings and programs of the African American college. In Mexico City's Colonia Station, Palmer is commemorated for building the Mexican National Railway from Laredo, Texas, to Mexico City with the support of the president of Mexico. And, in the Union Railroad Stations in Denver, Colorado, and in Salt Lake City, Utah, Palmer is praised for bringing the first railroads to the two cities from the east linking Denver and Salt Lake City with the well-established cities of the East and Midwest.

But there was more to Palmer's life than what the bronze tablets recount. Born in 1836 to John and Matilda Palmer in Delaware, William Jackson Palmer was raised as a Quaker and educated in Pennsylvania. At age 17, he became a civil engineer for the Pennsylvania Railroad and demonstrated his way-finding ability when he charted a route for the railroad over the Appalachian Mountains.

Though a Quaker, Palmer joined the Union Army during the Civil War because of his overriding belief that slavery should be abolished. He not only led troops, but also worked behind Confederate lines to find the best routes for Union soldiers and supplies to penetrate the South. Palmer was captured and spent several months as a prisoner of war before his eventual release. Before the

Civil War came to an end in 1865, Palmer was made Brigadier General.

After the war, Palmer headed west and founded the Denver and Rio Grande Railroad. Beginning in 1870, the railroad was built rail by rail until nearly 2,000 miles of track had been laid. Palmer's railroad linked mountain supply towns, such as Steamboat Springs, Alamosa, and Glenwood Springs, to many mining towns, including Silverton, Creede, and Aspen, to the fledgling cities of Denver, Colorado Springs, Pueblo, and Grand Junction.

Along the route of the Denver and Rio Grande, Palmer established the city of Colorado Springs, Alamosa, Durango, and other Colorado towns. Palmer's love of his hometown, Colorado Springs, is legendary. He donated more than 2,000 acres for parks, trails, and scenic drives, including Monument Valley Park, North Cheyenne Cañon Park, Acacia Park, and Palmer Park.

In a red rock canyon just north of Garden of the Gods, he built a castle patterned after elegant castles he had seen on trips to Europe, and, after selling his railroad, was able to enjoy his secluded estate. His Glen Eyrie Castle (pronounced Eye-rie) included a dairy farm, landscaped gardens, elaborate horse stables, and farmlands. He and his wife Mary Mellen Palmer, affectionately known as Queen, had three daughters.

Civil War general, pathfinder, engineer, railroad pioneer, benefactor, and city founder William Jackson Palmer will not be forgotten. The monuments to his life are evident every day in the hundreds of acres of donated parklands, in the railroads that still wind through the mountains, and in the colleges and cities that are thriving.

the mounted cowboys, the Range Riders.

To the left is the Antlers Doubletree Hotel. This is the third Antlers Hotel to be built in this location; the first two were built by Colorado Springs' founder, General William Jackson Palmer. The Palmer Center Plaza in front of the Antlers commemorates the general. From the day the Antlers Hotel opened until railway passenger service to Colorado Springs was discontinued, it was a very short walk or ride down the hill from Palmer's fashionable hotel to his Denver & Rio Grande Railroad Station—evidence of Palmer's thoughtful planning and good business sense.

Weldon Lee

The first hotel was built in 1883 and was named The Antlers for the deer and elk antlers that were part of the decor. After a fire destroyed the first Antlers, General Palmer built a lavish second hotel on the same location that opened in 1901. It framed Pikes Peak with its twin towers, and old-timers in the city still miss its turn-of-the-19th-century style. The third Antlers was built in 1967.

Mile 2.95. Turn left (west) almost immediately after the Antlers Hotel onto Pikes Peak Avenue.

Mile 3.1. Turn left (south) onto Sierra Madre Street.

Mile 3.2. Park at the metered parking on the street or in the Depot Shops parking area on the right. The old Denver & Rio Grande Railway Station, built in 1887, is now a restaurant. Lining the restaurant walls are many historic photographs of the gold camps of Cripple Creek and of the railroads during their heyday.

The first passenger train pulled into Colorado Springs on October 26, 1871, even before there was an official railroad station.

The Spotted Towhee
A Bird Who Sings Its Name

If a loud rustling sound in the scrub oak thicket startles you, chances are more likely that you've heard a spotted towhee than a large animal feeding in the shrubs. The colorful spotted towhee hops into the air and scratches in the dry leaves with both feet at the same time, using this noisy method to find seeds and insects to eat.

Because the towhee does not migrate, alert walkers and hikers have many opportunities to see this native bird. It is easy to identify with its black head, white breast, rust-colored sides, spotted wings, and red eyes. It is a bit smaller than a robin.

In the spring, the male towhee perches on the highest branch of a scrub oak or a mountain mahogany shrub and sings the same song over and over. The towhee was named for this repetitive song, a trilling *tow, tow, heeeee.* In spring and summer, listen for the towhee's trill whenever you walk in the foothills or natural parks. Year-round, you can hear the towhee rustling up "dinner" in the dry leaves.

The last passenger train to pull out of the station was in 1966. Several freight and coal trains still rumble through town every day.

Across the street from the Depot is Antlers Park where a Denver & Rio Grande Railroad engine is exhibited. After 50 years of continuous service, narrow-gauge engine 168 was retired and presented to the city of Colorado Springs. The venerable engine's claim to fame is that it pulled the first Denver & Rio Grande passenger train from Denver to Salt Lake City in 1883.

Leave the parking area, retrace your drive back north on Sierra Madre and continue north up the hill on Sierra Madre Street. Do not turn onto Pikes Peak Avenue. Sierra Madre converges with Kiowa Street.

Mile 3.5. Turn left (north) off Kiowa Street onto Cascade Avenue.

Mile 3.9. Look to the right at 423 North Cascade Avenue at the McAllister House Museum. This 1873 home was built by Winfield

Scott Stratton, who later struck it rich in Cripple Creek and gave up his carpentry trade. Stratton built the home for Henry and Elizabeth McAllister, following their directions to build the walls 20 inches thick to withstand the strong winds—called chinooks—that roar down from the mountains. Mr. McAllister was a friend and business partner of General Palmer's and served as a trustee of Colorado College for many years.

To the left on 506 N. Cascade Avenue is the gracious home where Alice Bemis Taylor grew up in the early 1900s. Mrs. Taylor financed the construction of and the endowment for the Colorado Springs Fine Arts Center.

Mile 4.2. Turn left on Dale Street, then into the Colorado Springs Fine Arts Center's parking lot on the left. When the Fine Arts Center was designed and built in 1936, its southwestern-style architecture was a bold departure from the western European and classical architecture of most of Colorado Springs' civic institutions. It features an unexpected, spacious outdoor courtyard in the center of the art galleries. The courtyard embraces the blue sky, introduces natural light into the galleries, and provides an inviting place for outdoor sculpture.

Built on the location of Julie and Spencer Penrose's first home, which became the Broadmoor Art Academy, the Fine Arts Center is not only an art museum, but also a center for theater, music, art education, and special annual events, such as the American Indian and Hispanic Marketplace and the Holiday Gallery of Trees. The appreciation that its founder, Alice Bemis Taylor, had for the architecture and people of the Southwest lives on at the Colorado Springs Fine Arts Center.

Opposite: Monument Valley Park provides serene spaces in downtown Colorado Springs.

Turn left out of the parking lot onto the one-way road and wind down the hill.

Mile 4.4. Turn right onto Mesa Street.

Mile 4.5. Turn left (west) onto Cache la Poudre Street and drive over the bridge.

Mile 4.6. Turn left into the parking lot at Monument Valley Park, a 2-mile-long city park donated by General Palmer and developed between 1904 and 1907. The shady picnic areas and walking paths, duck ponds and pavilions, tennis courts and swimming pool, playgrounds and flower gardens make Monument Valley one of the city's most popular recreation areas.

Mile 5.0. Turn left onto Uintah Street.

Mile 5.1. You are back to the intersection of Uintah Street and Interstate 25 where this tour began. In a short distance of 5 miles, you have traveled over several of Colorado Springs' original streets and have visited some of its historic parks and landmarks that are still vital to the city today.

9 Old Colorado City/Manitou Springs

Old Colorado City and Manitou Springs are both National Historic Districts lined with specialty shops, bakeries, and restaurants. A stroll along their tree-lined streets is a pleasant way to spend a day and soak up a little history along the way.

Old Colorado City is about halfway between downtown Colorado Springs and Manitou Springs, and is the oldest of the three communities. It was established in 1859 as Colorado City, and was a completely separate town from Colorado Springs until it was annexed in 1917. Old Colorado City, also called Old Town, retains and celebrates its distinct character and its special place in the history of the Pikes Peak region.

Manitou ("Springs" wasn't added to its name until 1935) was established in 1872 by Dr. William Bell, one of General William Jackson Palmer's business partners. Dr. Bell and General Palmer worked together to publicize their new towns, and Manitou soon was heralded as the "Saratoga of the West." The little town, nestled at the foot of Pikes Peak, had a special claim to fame with its unique bubbling soda and iron springs. Within only two years of its founding, Manitou boasted seven hotels and boarding houses as people flocked to the area seeking health from the soda springs and mountain air—both acclaimed for their curative powers.

Old Colorado City and Manitou Springs Tour

Total Mileage of Tour: 5.3 miles one-way

Mile 0.0. Begin this tour at the intersection of Interstate 25 and Highway 24 West, Interstate Exit 141. This is the designated Manitou Springs exit off Interstate 25. Drive west toward the mountains on Highway 24.

Mile 2.0. Turn right (north) onto 26th Street.

Mile 2.2. Turn right (east) onto Colorado Avenue.

Mile 2.5. Turn left (north) onto 24th Street and park in the lot of the Old Colorado City History Center at 1 South 24th Street. If the lot is full, several public parking lots are located behind the buildings lining Colorado Avenue and street parking is also available.

The Old Colorado History Center is the best introduction to Colorado City in the days between its founding in 1859 and when it was annexed by Colorado Springs in 1917. The History Center is housed in an 1890 building that was originally built as a church.

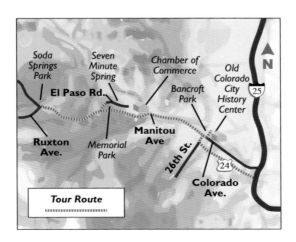

Weldon Lee

Weldon Lee

Chipmunks and Ground Squirrels

The closer you get to the foothills, the more likely you are to see these two small mammals. Chipmunks (pictured above) and ground squirrels are often spotted scurrying about during the warmer months and add a lot of motion to the landscape.

The 4-inch-long chipmunk, the smaller of the two, has dark brown and white stripes on its face extending from its nose to its ears. The ground squirrel has a small white circle around each eye, but no stripes on its face. The squirrel is about 7 inches long.

During the summer months, chipmunks and ground squirrels store part of their food supply of seeds, nuts, and berries. In late fall, they dig a burrow and hibernate for the winter. Then, in early spring when they emerge from hibernation, the chipmunks and ground squirrels live on their food cache until seeds and berries are plentiful once again. Even though these small mammals have similar seasonal routines, they live, collect food, and hibernate separately.

Historic photographs and artifacts, guided walking tours in the summer, and a well-stocked bookstore make the History Center, opened in 1997, a welcome addition to "Old Town."

Walk across 24th Street from the History Center to Bancroft Park. In the southwest corner of the park is a log cabin, the Pioneer County Office, which was built the year Colorado City was founded. In 1859, several members of a gold-prospecting party—including Anthony Bott, Melancthon Beach, and Rufus Cable—organized the Colorado City Town Company and established the town. This was two years before the Colorado Territory was created, 12 years before Colorado Springs was staked, and 17 years before Colorado became a state.

For a very brief time, only five days, Colorado City had the distinction of being the Colorado Territorial Capital. However, the legislators complained of inadequate lodging and lack of equipment and

Colorado Springs Pioneers Museum

Jane Root Quinby
Colorado City
Pioneer

Colorado City pioneer Jane Root Quinby faced many hardships, yet managed to cope and make a lasting contribution to her community. She and her husband Rodney moved to Colorado City in 1875 to establish their home and business. Jane had five children, but sadly, only one survived to adulthood. Rodney became a successful realtor with his partner, William Love. The partners developed and sold lots on the west side of Colorado City.

Rodney Quinby died in 1897, only 12 years after moving to Colorado City. Jane and her son Horace (pictured at Balanced Rock) continued the family's real estate business.

A founding member and trustee of the First Baptist Church of Colorado City, Jane Quinby donated the land for the church's first building. A handsome church was constructed and dedicated in 1890.

Today, the original church building that Jane Quinby helped finance serves as the Old Colorado City History Center, which documents and celebrates the intriguing history of "Old Town."

supplies, such as a printing press, and quickly decided to move the capital to Denver.

Nevertheless, Colorado City thrived as a trade center for the mining camps farther west, and as a stage stop on the stage line between Denver and Santa Fe. When it was linked by railroad to Cripple Creek, it became an essential hub in gold mining enterprises with the establishment of five huge gold processing mills.

As you walk the Historic District along Colorado Avenue between 24th Street and 27th Street, there are several historic buildings of note, including the Waycott Opera House at 2432 West Colorado and the 1891 Dry Goods Building at 2504 West Colorado.

Drive west on Colorado Avenue toward the mountains to resume the driving tour.

Below: Cozy Manitou Springs nestles in the foothills.

Weldon Lee

Set your odometer to 0.0 at the intersection of Colorado Avenue and 26th Street.

Mile 1.4. You will drive under the Manitou Springs welcome arch that marks the Manitou Springs city limits. Here, Colorado Avenue becomes Manitou Avenue. All along Manitou Avenue, quaint motels and cottages usually post their No Vacancy signs for part of every summer as vacationers flock to Colorado.

Mile 1.9. Just after Manitou Avenue leads under the Highway 24 bridge, the Manitou Springs public swimming pool and shaded

Steller's Jay
The Mountain Blue Jay

It is hard to miss this raucous jay with its bright, royal-blue color and black-crested head. The Steller's jay has the longest crest of any North American bird. Up close, you can see white streaks of feathers over its eyes that look like eyebrows.

The jay lives year-round in Colorado's evergreen forests, and usually nests at 6,500 to 8,000 feet in elevation. Like all jays, the Steller's eats mostly seeds, nuts, berries, and insects, but occasionally will eat bird eggs and small rodents.

The Steller's jay was named by Georg Steller, a German zoologist, who collected the jay on a scientific expedition to Alaska in 1741. This jay is very widespread and thrives in the mountainous forests from Alaska all the way south to Guatemala.

Watch for this handsome bird on the fringes of Manitou Springs, where the town meets the mountains.

park are in view to the right.

Mile 2.3. Stop at the Manitou Springs Chamber of Commerce at 354 Manitou Avenue if you need any additional maps or information. A free map of the exact location of Manitou's soda springs is available.

Mile 2.8. Turn right onto El Paso Boulevard and park in the marked spaces along Memorial Park. The park is bordered on the south by Fountain Creek and on the north by the Victorian gazebo of Seven Minute Spring, one of the town's nine restored springs. In 1987, the Mineral Springs Foundation was established to maintain and mark the historic springs. You will see several of the mineral springs as you walk along Manitou Avenue. The water of the drinking springs can be sampled by the public at no charge.

From Memorial Park to the west end of the Manitou Springs downtown area is 0.4 mile one-way. It can be either walked or driven. During the summer months, you can wave down and ride the open-air Town Trolley that cruises the town for a small fee. The

The Palsgrove Family
Hardworking Homesteaders

In late May 1884, Tom and Nettie Palsgrove packed up their six-week-old baby daughter, four-year-old son, and all their possessions, then set out with Nettie's mother from Manitou to their new home in the mountains. Riding on plodding burros, they followed a narrow path 3 miles up Englemann Canyon to their 160-acre homesteading claim. Tom's plan was to enlarge the tiny cabin for his family and to begin a small cattle ranch.

The first part of Tom's plan, to build additions onto the cabin, worked well, but his cattle ranching effort at 9,000 feet in elevation was a complete failure. Most of the cattle died during a huge spring snowstorm.

Fortunately, Tom found

Colorado Springs Pioneers Museum

other ways to make a living. He took advantage of the unique location of his property, as the trail from Manitou to the summit of Pikes Peak crossed his land. Just a year after settling into their home, the Palsgroves began to take in overnight guests who were climbing Pikes Peak. Soon, the Palsgrove place was known as Halfway House, and Tom began to add more rooms.

Between 1884 and 1892, all three of Tom's younger brothers moved from Pennsylvania to Colorado to work on Tom's enterprise and to stake their own homestead claims. They kept building onto Halfway House until it could accommodate 50 overnight guests. And the Palsgrove brothers added acreage to their homesteads until they owned more than 600 acres on Pikes Peak's eastern slopes.

By the late 1880s, the thriving resort of Manitou had at least a dozen hotels, and many offered burro rides to the top of Pikes Peak. Some featured "sunrise" trips, where tourists rode to Halfway House on the first day, slept for a few hours, then continued their burro ride in the dark early morning hours so they could watch the sunrise from Pikes Peak's summit.

When the cog railway was completed in 1891, it featured a stop at Halfway House. Eventually, the more hectic pace at Halfway House influenced Tom and Nettie to turn over the management of the hotel to Tom's brother John. Tom and his family moved to Grand Junction, Colorado, while John's family continued to operate Halfway House until 1916, when the popular landmark closed. (Pictured: Tom and John Palsgrove.)

Town Trolley drivers double as tour guides of the area.

Proceeding west from Seven Minute Spring and Memorial Park, you will first see an 1893 train locomotive that operated for 46 years on the Manitou and Pikes Peak Railway. Pikes Peak, 14,110 feet, looms above the west end of town, and the cog railway to its summit starts off from Manitou Springs.

As you walk west toward the mountains on Manitou Avenue, it will become apparent that Manitou Springs is a mecca for artists. Art galleries and outdoor sculpture decorate the small town inside and out.

Continue west on Manitou Avenue for 0.2 mile and you will cross Cañon Avenue. This narrow street is lined with art galleries and eateries and is just across from the town clock, a local landmark.

Continue west on Manitou Avenue for 0.1 mile to the Manitou Arcade. The Arcade is a 1930s addition to the town and offers nostalgic amusement such as skee ball, pinball machines, and coin-operated rides for

Above: Cañon Avenue is a favorite place to shop and dine in Manitou Springs.

youngsters. An afternoon of eating soft ice cream cones and caramel corn while strolling along Manitou Avenue will remind you what vacations are all about.

Continue west on Manitou Avenue for 0.1 mile to Soda Springs Park, which features a children's playground, picnic tables, and a covered pavilion. Walk across Manitou Avenue at this location, and you will see Ruxton Avenue, which leads to the Pikes Peak Cog Railway Station. As you walk the 0.4 mile back to Memorial Park, enjoy the mountain air, sips of mineral water, and the views just as visitors did over a century ago.

The Wild Geranium

The fragile, pink petals of the wild geranium are so thin they are almost transparent. Sunlight makes these wildflowers seem to glow.

Wild geraniums usually bloom in mid-July, adding color to the mountain meadows and the edges of the forests. After pollination, the geranium's seedpods grow to about 1 inch in length. These elongated, beaklike seedpods are the reason for the geranium's other common name, crane's bill.

Air Force Academy

W hen the United States Air Force Academy opened in 1958, it joined the academies of the Army (West Point, New York), Navy (Annapolis, Maryland), Coast Guard (New London, Connecticut), and Merchant Marine (Long Island, New York). Today, the Air Force Academy, just north of Colorado Springs, is the country's fifth and youngest military academy.

In 1947, shortly after World War II, the United States Air Force was established as a separate military service. A few years later, when President Dwight D. Eisenhower signed the legislation for the construction of an academy for the Air Force, more than 500 proposed sites in 45 states were considered. Each site competed for the honor, prestige, and economic benefit that the academy would bring.

The Colorado Springs location rose to the top, and once you visit the Academy, it is apparent that it was the right choice. The spacious setting of the Academy's 19,000 acres borders the Rampart Range. The Academy's immense buildings seem in proportion to the mountains in the background.

At 7,200 feet in elevation, the Academy is a lofty place for 4,000 cadets to learn how to be leaders in the Air Force. Visitors are welcome to tour the Academy's thoughtfully designed campus, and to learn more about the Air Force and its history.

The United States Air Force Academy Tour

Total Mileage of Tour: 12.1 miles

Directions to the beginning of the tour: This tour begins at the north entrance to the Air Force Academy as it is the more scenic and the more direct route to the most interesting sites.

Take Interstate 25 north from Colorado Springs to Exit 156 B, the Academy's North Gate/Gleneagle Exit. After exiting, drive west on North Gate Road toward the mountains. The Air Force Academy is plainly in view with its silver buildings lining the base of the foothills.

On the right, just before reaching the Academy entry station, is the parking lot of the New Santa Fe Regional Trail, a 14-mile walking and mountain biking trail.

Set your odometer to 0.0 at the entry station. Drive slowly through the station and be prepared to stop if the guard indicates.

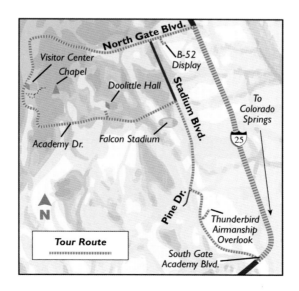

Scrub Jay
The Tree Planter

Like ravens and magpies, jays are members of the crow family and have similar traits. All have raucous calls, tend to live in small family flocks, and are considered among the most intelligent birds.

Scrub jays are easy to identify by their colors—blue head, tail, and wings; white throat, light breast, and gray back. Unlike the Steller's jay, the scrub jay has a sleek head rather than a crest.

Scrub jays are most often found in scrub oak thickets in the foothills. It is only during the breeding season that the word "secretive" would describe this jay. For the rest of the year, the bird's noisy call and flash of blue feathers usually herald its location.

When acorns have developed on the scrub oak trees, the scrub jays go to work preparing for winter. You can watch a scrub jay gather an acorn, then fly to a particular location to store the acorn for the winter. Using its sturdy beak, the jay pushes the acorn into the ground, effectively hiding it for future use, and inadvertently planting a tree.

Weldon Lee

Below: Eagle Peak provides a scenic backdrop for the U.S. Air Force Academy.

There is no entry fee. Be sure to note the posted speed limit throughout the Academy.

Mile 0.6. Make two left-hand turns into the parking lot of the B-52 Bomber exhibit if you wish to view the bomber up close. The wingspan of this huge airplane is longer than half a football field. Detailed information about the bomber is exhibited near its base.

Turn right out of the parking lot back to North Gate Road. Turn left on North Gate Road and follow the signs to the Visitor Center. North Gate Road becomes Academy Drive as you proceed to the next stop.

Colorado Historical Society

Dr. Edwin James
Expedition Doctor and Botanist

In 1820, Major Stephen Long led an expedition to continue the exploration of the Louisiana Purchase, which the United States had bought from France in 1803. Major Long was commissioned to explore the source of the Platte River, then return along the Arkansas and Red Rivers back to the Mississippi.

Major Long asked Dr. Edwin James, a 22-year-old doctor and botanist, to join his expedition to provide medical services and to describe the plants and landmarks found along the way. On June 6, Long's small expedition left the Missouri River, heading west along the Platte River with 22 men and 28 pack animals.

Upon reaching the Front Range of the Rockies, Dr. James began to collect many plants that had never been described by botanists. Just a few miles north of today's Air Force Academy, Dr. James collected the first columbine flower known to science.

The young botanist also convinced Major Long to halt the expedition for three days so that he could try to climb the Grand Peak (Pikes Peak). On July 13, Dr. James and two climbing companions, baggage master Zachariah Wilson and Private Joseph Verplank, began the long climb. Nightfall forced them to camp overnight and to resume their climb early the next morning. Excerpts from James's detailed journal describe their July 14 ascent:

> Above the point where the timber disappears . . . commences a region of astonishing beauty. . . . It was about 4 o'clock p.m. when we arrived on the summit. . . . the view towards the north, west and southwest is diversified with innumerable mountains, all white with snow.

To honor James and his successful climb, Major Long named the high mountain James Peak on his expedition map. However, the name Pikes Peak was more widely used and eventually won out.

Nevertheless, the energetic botanist has not been forgotten. Dr. James's grand adventure placed him in the history books for achieving the first recorded climb of Pikes Peak, which was also the first recorded climb of any 14,000-foot peak in the continental United States. James is also listed in botanical journals for being the first scientist to describe the high-altitude tundra flowers of the Rocky Mountains.

In Colorado, a 13,294-foot mountain on the Continental Divide is named after Edwin James, and the blue columbine was selected as Colorado's official state flower. Its scientific name is *Aquilegia caerulea James*.

Mile 1.5. The scenic overlook features a view of the entire Academy with the cadet athletic fields in the foreground. The next overlook provides an even better view.

Mile 1.8. This overlook offers a grassy terrace and benches to take in the scene. A memorial commemorates the first Air Force Chief of Staff, General Carl Andrew Spaatz, and a numbered photo exhibit identifies and describes the Academy buildings viewed from this site.

Mile 3.6. The Air Force Academy Visitor Center features excellent exhibits and a movie about Academy life, academics, athletics, and other programs. A staffed information booth, snack bar, and

Weldon Lee

Mule Deer
The Region's Most Common Large Mammal

Mule deer are often seen in the local foothills, mountains, natural parks—and in many residents' backyards. The graceful animals are easy to identify with their large, mulelike ears and black-tipped tail. They are most active at night as they seek water and browse on bushes, twigs, and sometimes flower gardens.

Only the male deer grow antlers, which are composed of solid bone and are shed every year. Horns, such as those found on bighorn sheep, are hollow inside and are not shed. The mule deer sheds its antlers in the winter, and begins growing a new set in the spring. The new antlers are covered by "velvet," a furry skin. The velvet contains blood vessels and protects the tender antlers. When the antlers have attained their annual growth, the deer rubs off the velvet just in time for the fall breeding season.

Look for mule deer or their tracks whenever you walk, hike, or mountain bike in the Pikes Peak region. And be alert for deer running across roads and highways whenever you drive. Deer are particularly abundant in the natural open spaces surrounding the Air Force Academy.

large gift shop are also available. During the summer, free guided tours and planetarium shows are offered daily. Times are posted at the Visitor Center. You may want to call ahead and listen to the recorded information line at 719-333-USAF. Self-guided maps are available year-round at the Visitor Center information booth.

Picnickers are welcome to eat on the Center's spacious, south-facing deck. It has a great view of Eagle Peak where peregrine falcons have been reintroduced in recent years. Watch the skies for Academy airplanes and gliders, as well as for falcons.

The one-third mile trail leading from the Visitor Center to the Air

Force Academy Chapel is well worth the short walk. The trail winds through beautiful ponderosa pines, offering stunning views of the Academy Chapel. Along the trail are wayside exhibits describing some of the most common plants and wildlife that are native to the foothills of the Academy.

The Air Force Academy Chapel is one of the most visited sites in all of Colorado. Once you step inside, you will understand why. The intense blues of the stained-glass windows seem suspended in space, and the silver walls seem to soar as they intersect 150 feet overhead.

On the east side of the Chapel is an exhibit that identifies the cadet buildings. Each is named in honor of heroic people in Air Force history. On the northwest side of the Chapel is Harmon Hall Courtyard, which features bronze sculptures of Air Force heroes and airplanes.

If you are physically unable to make the walk to the Chapel from the Visitor Center, you may drive to the closer visitor and handicapped parking area. Ask at the Visitor Center information booth for specific directions.

Reset your odometer to 0.0 when you leave the Visitor Center parking lot.

Mile 2.1. Doolittle Hall is a privately financed and operated building serving as the Academy's alumni headquarters. It is open to the public on most weekdays and contains exhibits, artwork, and a gift shop.

Mile 4.1. Turn right onto Stadium Boulevard. You will pass the Air Force Academy Falcon Stadium, the location of all home football games and cadet graduation.

Mile 6.2. Bear left around the curve, cross over Monument Creek, and follow the signs to the South Gate Entry/Interstate 25.

Mile 6.8. The Thunderbird Airmanship Overlook offers views of practice flights, takeoffs, and landings as cadets learn to pilot airplanes and gliders. Parachute jumping is also practiced in this area. The jet on exhibit is a Thunderbird. These sleek jets and

John Fielder

Indian Paintbrush

Indian paintbrushes are the brightest wildflowers of summer. They really do look like paintbrushes dipped in bright-colored paint, then set out into the meadows to dry. Indian paintbrushes in the foothills are usually red or orange in color. At higher altitudes, paintbrushes in shades of rose and yellow are more common.

their ace pilots perform at air shows around the nation and around the world.

Mile 8.5. The circle tour of the Air Force Academy ends at its South Entry Gate near Interstate 25. If you need to drive north, follow the signs to Denver. If you are heading south, follow the signs to Colorado Springs.

Below: More than one million visitors come to view the soaring spires of the Academy's chapel each year.

The Prairie Falcon
An Intimidating Predator

The prairie falcon is built for speed. Its shape is entirely streamlined with a sleek head, long pointed wings, and a tapered tail. These features enable the prairie falcon to overtake its favored prey of swifts and rock doves and snatch them out of the air.

Another hunting technique of this bird of prey is "stooping." Flying at great heights, the prairie falcon targets a bird, then folds its wings and dives at 200 miles per hour to strike its prey with such tremendous force that it knocks the prey out of the air.

In the Pikes Peak area, prairie falcons can usually be found year-round in the cliffs and canyons of the foothills. In recent years, they have successfully nested in the towering rocks of Garden of the Gods Park. Close observers may see rock doves and white-throated swifts scatter when a prairie falcon takes to the air.

U.S. Air Force Academy

The fast-flying falcon is the mascot of the Air Force Academy, and several are raised and trained at the Academy.

Agency Contacts
in the Pikes Peak Region (partial listing)

National

**Florissant Fossil Beds
National Monument**
15807 County Road 1
Florissant, Colorado 80816
719-748-3253

Pike National Forest
601 S. Weber Street
Colorado Springs, Colorado
80903
719-636-1602

San Isabel National Forest
1920 Valley Drive
Pueblo, Colorado 81008
719-545-8737

State

**State of Colorado
Division of Wildlife,
Regional Office**
2126 N. Weber Street
Colorado Springs, Colorado
80907
719-473-2945

**Colorado State Patrol, Road
and Weather Conditions**
719-630-1111

Mueller Ranch State Park
P.O. Box 49
Divide, Colorado 80814
719-687-2366

**Pueblo State Recreation
Area**
640 Pueblo Reservoir Drive
Pueblo, Colorado 81005
719-561-9320

County

**El Paso County Regional
Parks Main Office**
2002 Creek Crossing
Colorado Springs, Colorado
80906
719-520-6375

Bear Creek Nature Center
245 Bear Creek Road
Colorado Springs, Colorado
80906
719-520-6387

**Fountain Creek Nature
Center**
320 Pepper Grass Lane
Colorado Springs, Colorado
80911
719-520-6745

Colorado Springs

**Colorado Springs Parks
and Recreation
Department, Main Office**
1401 Recreation Way
Colorado Springs, Colorado
80905
719-578-6640

**Beidleman Environmental
Center**
740 W. Caramillo
Colorado Springs, Colorado
80907
719-578-7088

**Garden of the Gods
Visitor Center**
1805 N. 30th Street
Colorado Springs, Colorado
80904
719-634-6666

**Helen Hunt Falls Visitor
Center**
3340 N. Cheyenne Cañon Road
Colorado Springs, Colorado
80906
719-634-9320

**Rock Ledge Ranch
Historic Site**
3202 Chambers Way
Colorado Springs, Colorado
80904
719-578-6777

Starsmore Discovery Center
2120 S. Cheyenne Cañon Road
Colorado Springs, Colorado
80906
719-578-6146

Pueblo

**Greenway and Nature
Center of Pueblo**
5200 Nature Center Road
Pueblo, Colorado 81003
719-549-2414

**Pueblo Parks and
Recreation Department**
800 Goodnight Avenue
Pueblo, Colorado 81005
719-566-1745

Natural and Historic Attractions
in the Pikes Peak Region

Visitor Information

Cañon City Chamber of Commerce
P.O. Bin 749-Z
Cañon City, Colorado 81215
719-275-2331

Colorado Springs Convention and Visitors Bureau
104 S. Cascade Avenue
Colorado Springs, Colorado 80903
719-635-7506

Manitou Springs Chamber of Commerce and Pikes Peak Country Attractions
354 Manitou Avenue
Manitou Springs, Colorado 80829
719-685-5089

Pueblo Chamber of Commerce
302 N. Santa Fe Avenue
Pueblo, Colorado 81003
1-800-233-3446

Attractions

Cave of the Winds
Manitou Springs, Colorado 80829
719-685-5444

Cheyenne Mountain Zoo
4250 Cheyenne Mountain Zoo Road
Colorado Springs, Colorado 80906
719-633-9925

Colorado Springs Fine Arts Center
30 W. Dale Street
Colorado Springs, Colorado 80903
719-634-5581

Colorado Springs Pioneers Museum
215 S. Tejon Street
Colorado Springs, Colorado 80903
719-578-6650

Cripple Creek District Museum
Bennett Avenue
Cripple Creek, Colorado 80813
719-689-2640

Cripple Creek and Victor Narrow Gauge Railroad
5th and Carr Avenue
Cripple Creek, Colorado 80813
719-689-2640

Dinosaur Depot
330 Royal Gorge Boulevard
Cañon City, Colorado 81212
1-800-987-6379

El Pueblo Museum
324 W. 1st Street
Pueblo, Colorado 81003
719-583-0453

Garden of the Gods Trading Post
324 Beckers Lane
Manitou Springs, Colorado 80829
719-685-9045

Garden of the Gods Visitor Center
1805 N. 30th Street
Colorado Springs, Colorado 80904
719-634-6666

Manitou and Pikes Peak Cog Railway
515 Ruxton Avenue
Manitou Springs, Colorado 80829
719-685-5401

Mollie Kathleen Mine
Highway 67
Cripple Creek, Colorado 80813
719-689-2465

Old Colorado City History Center
1 S. 24th Street
Colorado Springs, Colorado 80904
719-636-1225

Pikes Peak Highway
Highway 24 and Pikes Peak Highway
Cascade, Colorado 80809
719-684-9383

ProRodeo Hall of Fame
101 ProRodeo Drive
Colorado Springs, Colorado 80919
719-528-4764

Rosemount Victorian House Museum
419 W. 14th Street
Pueblo, Colorado 81003
719-545-5290

Royal Gorge
Highway 50
Cañon City, Colorado 81215
719-275-7507

Sangre de Cristo Arts and Conference Center
210 N. Santa Fe Avenue
Pueblo, Colorado 81003
719-432-0130

Seven Falls
South Cheyenne Cañon Road
Colorado Springs, Colorado 80906
719-632-0752

United States Air Force Academy Visitor Center
Academy Drive
USAF Academy, Colorado 80840
719-333-8723

Western Museum of Mining and Industry
1025 Northgate Road
Colorado Springs, Colorado 80921
719-488-0880

Source Material and Recommended Reading

Benedict, Audrey DeLella. *A Sierra Club Naturalist's Guide, The Southern Rockies.* Sierra Club Books, San Francisco, California, 1991.

Bright, William. *Colorado Place Names.* Johnson Books, Boulder, Colorado, 1993.

Brown, Jesse, Jr. and J. Christine Brown. *History: Payne Chapel African Methodist Episcopal Church 1872-1997.* Colorado Annual Conference Proceedings, Payne Chapel, Colorado Springs, Colorado, 1997.

Brunk, Ivan W. *Pike's Peak Pioneers.* Little London Press, Colorado Springs, Colorado, 1989.

Carson, Phil. *Among the Eternal Snows: The First Recorded Ascent of Pikes Peak.* First Ascent Press, Colorado Springs, Colorado, 1995.

Chronic, Halka. *Roadside Geology of Colorado.* Mountain Press Publishing Company, Missoula, Montana, 1980.

Coues, Elliott. *The Expeditions of Zebulon Montgomery Pike.* Dover Publications, Inc., New York, New York, 1987.

Daniels, Bettie Marie and Virginia McConnell. *The Springs of Manitou.* Manitou Springs Historical Society, Manitou Springs, Colorado, 1982.

Delaney, Robert W., James Jefferson, Floyd A. O'Neil and Gregory C. Thompson. *The Southern Utes: A Tribal History.* University of Utah Printing Service, Salt Lake City, Utah, 1973.

Evans, Howard Ensign. *Pioneer Naturalists.* Henry Holt and Company, Inc., New York, New York, 1993.

Gordon, Joseph T. and Judith A. Pickle. *Helen Hunt Jackson's Colorado.* The Hulbert Center for Southwestern Studies, Colorado College, Colorado Springs, Colorado, 1989.

Guennel, G. K. *A Guide to Colorado Wildflowers, Volumes 1 and 2.* Westcliffe Publishers, Englewood, Colorado, 1995.

Hershey, Charlie Brown. *Colorado College 1874-1949.* Dentan Printing Company, Colorado Springs, Colorado, 1952.

Holley, John Stokes. *The Invisible People of the Pikes Peak Region.* Friends of the Colorado Springs Pioneers Museum, Colorado Springs, Colorado, 1990.

Jenkins, John T. and Jannice L. Jenkins. *Colorado's Dinosaurs.* Colorado Geologic Survey, Denver, Colorado, 1993.

Johnson, Emily. *The White House Ranch.* O'Brien Printing and Lithographic Press, 1972.

Knox, Jan. *Jane Root Quinby*. West Word: Old Colorado City Historical Society, Colorado Springs, Colorado, November 1995.

Kohl, Michael and John S. McIntosh. *Discovering Dinosaurs in the Old West: The Field Journals of Arthur Lakes*. Smithsonian Institution Press, Washington, D.C., 1997.

Kruger, Frances Alley and Carron A. Meaney. *Explore Colorado, A Naturalist's Notebook*. Denver Museum of Natural History and Westcliffe Publishing, Englewood, Colorado, 1995.

Lee, Storrs W. *Colorado: A Literary Chronicle*. Funk and Wagnalls, New York, 1970.

Noblett, Jeffrey B. *A Guide to the Geological History of the Pikes Peak Region*. Colorado College Geology Department, Colorado Springs, Colorado, 1994.

Noel, Thomas J. and Duane A. Smith. *Colorado, The Highest State*. University Press of Colorado, Niwot, Colorado, 1995.

Oldach, Denise R. W. and Mary C. Claypool. *Here Lies Colorado Springs*. City of Colorado Springs, Evergreen and Fairview Cemeteries, Colorado Springs, Colorado, 1995.

Onis, Jose de. *The Hispanic Contribution to the State of Colorado*. Westview Press, Inc., Boulder, Colorado, 1976.

Peabody, George Foster. *William Jackson Palmer: Pathfinder and Builder*. Thomas Todd Company, Boston, Massachusetts, 1931.

Pettit, Jan. *Ute Pass*. Little London Press, Colorado Springs, Colorado, 1979.

Rennicke, Jeff. *Colorado Wildlife*. Colorado Division of Wildlife and Falcon Press Publishing Company, Inc., Helena and Billings, Montana, 1990.

Robbins, Chandler S., Bertel Bruun and Herbert S. Zim. *Birds of North America*. Golden Press, Western Publishing Company, Wisconsin, 1966.

Robertson, Janet. *The Magnificent Mountain Women*. University of Nebraska Press, 1990.

Sprague, Marshall. *Newport in the Rockies*. Swallow Press/Ohio University Press, 1987.

Spring, Agnes Wright. *A Bloomer Girl on Pike's Peak 1858*. Denver Public Library, 1949.

Terres, John K. *The Audubon Society Encyclopedia of North American Birds*. Alfred A. Knopf, New York, New York, 1980.

Wilcox, Rhoda. *The Man On The Iron Horse*. Martin Associates, Manitou Springs, Colorado, 1996.

Zwinger, Ann H. and Beatrice E. Willard. *Land Above the Trees*. Johnson Publishing, Boulder, Colorado, 1996.

Melissa Walker grew up in north Louisiana and enjoyed summer vacations in the West. She received her B.A. and M.A. degrees from Colorado College and has worked for over fifteen years as a lead park naturalist in the Pikes Peak region at Bear Creek Nature Center, Beidleman Environmental Center, and Garden of the Gods Park, presenting programs and developing park master plans and exhibits. Melissa now owns her own business, Envision, and specializes in natural history writing and park exhibit planning. She lives in Colorado Springs with her husband and son.